Sunset

Tax$aver
Itemized
Deductions

By Jay Knepp, CPA
Tax Specialist

S0-EAU-392

Lane Publishing Co. ■ Menlo Park, California

Edited by Fran Feldman
Coordinating Editor: Linda Selden
Design: Brooklyn Graphic
Cover Design: Design Systems Group

Sunset Books
  Editor: David E. Clark
  Managing Editor: Elizabeth L. Hogan

First printing January 1987

From Coopers & Lybrand

We have reviewed *Itemized Deductions Tax$aver* for accuracy in its description of federal income tax law.

Based on our interpretation of the Internal Revenue Code (including 1986 amendments) and its regulations, public rulings, and court decisions, we believe that *Tax$aver* accurately describes and interprets the applicable provisions of the law. Any taxpayer who follows the guidance of *Tax$aver* will have appropriate documentation to support his or her itemized deductions.

However, it is important to recognize that federal income tax laws and application of the Internal Revenue Service code and regulations are often a matter of interpretation. As a result, an Internal Revenue Service agent examining a taxpayer's return may disagree with the treatment of certain items of income and deductions as covered in this book. Because tax laws are continually subject to change by legislation, Internal Revenue Service regulations, public rulings, and court decisions, we cannot guarantee that a position taken by a taxpayer based on information in this book will not be successfully challenged by the Internal Revenue Service. In addition, individual facts and circumstances may result in an outcome different from that anticipated.

In view of the complexities of the tax laws and varying interpretations, taxpayers should not rely solely on the advice contained in *Tax$aver*, but should use it in conjunction with advice from their own tax advisor.

(Coopers & Lybrand is an international accounting firm with 98 offices in the United States.)

Table of Contents

Contents (Cont'd.)

If you are among the many taxpayers who itemize their deductions on Schedule A and attach it to their return, then *Itemized Deductions Tax$aver* is for you. It's a unique combination of tax advice and information plus a systematic record-keeping system designed to give the IRS the records and documentation it demands—and, in some cases, even more.

This book, specifically created with itemized deductions in mind, is designed for *you*, not for a tax specialist. It contains complete tax information on the situations you might encounter when filing Schedule A and tells you what you can deduct, how to keep required records easily and simply, and how to prove your claims should you be audited. Changes resulting from the Tax Reform Act of 1986 are highlighted in the text.

Above all, the book helps you minimize your taxes by showing you how to claim each and every deduction you deserve—the ultimate goal of all taxpayers.

Claiming Schedule A Deductions

Schedule A deductions include medical and dental expenses, taxes, interest, charitable contributions, casualty and theft losses, moving expenses, and a category called miscellaneous. Each deduction is discussed in detail in a separate section of the book, followed immediately by all the forms you'll need to keep track of that particular deduction.

Each year, it gets harder and harder to claim these deductions. First, the new tax law increases the standard deduction available to all taxpayers, which makes it less attractive to itemize. Second, because limitations apply to several of the deductions, it's essential to keep complete records to maximize and prove that you're entitled to the deductions you're claiming.

Medical and dental expenses must be related to the treatment and prevention of disease, physical or mental, to qualify as a deduction. Your expenses

5

must be reduced by any reimbursements you receive, and beginning in 1987, your deduction is limited to the amount of your expenses that exceeds 7½% (formerly 5%) of your adjusted gross income.

Taxes you can deduct may include income taxes, real estate taxes, and personal property taxes. Sales taxes are no longer deductible under the Tax Reform Act of 1986.

Interest, including home mortgage interest, investment mortgage, and below-market interest rate loans, is also deductible, but may be subject to limitations and exceptions. Under the new law, consumer interest deductions are being phased out.

Charitable contributions, whether they're made in cash or in property, are subject to strict rules. Again, there are limitations to your deduction, and you can only deduct contributions to certain qualified organizations.

Casualty and theft losses, though usually covered by insurance, are deductible when they exceed 10% of adjusted gross income and if proper valuations of the loss are determined and substantiated.

Moving expenses are now deductible only as an itemized deduction, under the provisions of the Tax Reform Act of 1986. Limitations apply to certain types of expenses, and time and distance tests must be met.

Miscellaneous deductions encompass a wide range of other allowable deductions. Among them are unreimbursed employee business expenses and expenses of producing income. Only the amount of all miscellaneous deductions that exceeds 2% of adjusted gross income is deductible.

Be sure to consult the checklists that appear near the end of the sections. They'll tell you at a glance which expenses are deductible and which are not.

The Importance Of Good Records

Good records will help you prove not only the amount and type of each expenditure but also its actual character, decisive in determining whether or not it's a valid deduction. With such records, it will also be easier to fill out your return.

If your tax return is selected for an audit and

certain deductions are challenged by the IRS, it's usually up to you to prove that you're entitled to claim them. With this book, you'll be armed not only with knowledge but also with excellent documentation for all your itemized deductions.

Permanent annual records. The tax information and forms included in this book are designed for one year's use. The reasons for this are simple and logical. Tax laws change constantly and starting a new book each year enables you to keep up to date with changes in tax law, as well as current developments. It reduces the chance you'll waste time and energy keeping records that are no longer required, or fail to meet some new requirement, which could prove costly. Also, with a permanent annual record, you'll always be prepared if the IRS audits your return.

Keeping abreast of tax law. Laws and regulations pertaining to itemized deductions change rapidly and often. In addition, court decisions are continually influencing and reinterpreting tax law. Be aware, however, that certain court decisions aren't binding in all jurisdictions.

But many areas in tax law are simply too complex for the average taxpayer. It's always wise to consult a competent professional tax advisor about any situation that concerns you, especially where large amounts of money are involved. For this reason, we've included a section to help you choose a competent professional tax advisor.

Tax terms. Baffled by the complicated terms used by the IRS in their tax forms and publications? In order to comply with all the regulations, it's essential to understand and speak their language. For definitions of the most commonly used tax terms, consult the glossary beginning on page 140. ■

Record-Keeping & Substantiation Requirements

Whether you're preparing your own tax return, turning your records over to a professional tax advisor, or facing an audit by the IRS, complete tax records maintained in an orderly, organized fashion are essential.

Clearly, if you want to deduct certain expenses and thereby reduce your tax bill, you're going to have to maintain records which substantiate your claims. It's no secret that many taxpayers regard this work as tedious and unpleasant. But once you know what constitutes good records and how to keep them, and you understand how to use the specially designed forms in this book (all of which meet current IRS record-keeping requirements), you can claim your deductions with ease and confidence.

What are adequate records? The IRS does not require you to keep records in any particular form or by any special method. They say only that you must have adequate records and sufficient evidence which, in combination, can establish the amount, date, and nature of all income items, deductions, and credits claimed on your return. Receipts which show the essential character of the expense are ordinarily the best evidence to prove your deductions. Record the date and amount of each expense, along with a brief description.

These records should be permanent, accurate, complete, and supported by any documents that clearly establish the nature and intent of the expense. Remember, however, that any record or evidence is not the sole determinant of deductibility. The facts and circumstances of each case will often dictate the final tax result.

How elaborate your records are depends on your individual situation. However, canceled checks alone are not usually considered as proper proof when unsupported by other documentary evidence.

When to make entries. Except for employee business expenses, the IRS doesn't require that you maintain a record made at or near the time the expense occurs for most itemized deductions. It's up to you to decide when it's most suitable for you to make entries. If you have a lot of transactions, recording them weekly may be necessary. Most taxpayers, however, can make monthly entries. Whatever time frame you choose, develop a routine and stick to it.

How to keep good records. This book provides all the specific instructions and forms you'll need for all itemized deductions. Keep it in a convenient place and don't rely on memory—it's easy to forget incidental expenses.

Tax$aver Tip. *An excellent way to keep track of all deductible expenses, regardless of how paid, is to invest in a portable tape recorder. That way, you can tape-record your activities and expenses during the week, and then enter all the information in this book at a later date.*

Here are some additional hints which may be of help:

- Always pay by check or credit card if possible, since you're instantly creating a useful record.
- Always ask for a receipt, especially when paying cash, and keep all receipts on file.
- When you can't get a receipt for a cash payment, record and explain the payment in your records as soon as possible.
- Except for incidental expenses, which can be combined daily, your expenses should generally be recorded separately.

How long to retain records. All logs, checkbooks, canceled checks, receipts, and tax returns should be retained for at least 3 years from the date of filing; that's the usual length of time the IRS may select a return for audit. However, if it's found that some income was not reported and it's greater than 25% of what was reported, the period available for audit is 6 years after the return was filed. And the IRS can go back to *any* year when no return is filed, a return is false or fraudulent, or criminal activity is suspected.

The following records should be retained indefinitely:

1. Records that relate to the basis of your home or any property subject to depreciation and that are needed to figure either the gain or loss when the asset is sold or the basis of new property when a trade-in is involved
2. Property records required to figure the amount of depreciation or investment tax credit recapture due to sale or disposition of business property before the end of its estimated recovery period

You'll also need records from prior years if you file a claim for a refund for taxes you've overpaid, if you need to amend a prior year's return, or if changes in tax law entitle you to benefits only on the basis of previous years' records. Often, records can also be helpful to the executor of your estate.

To obtain a copy of a prior year's return, ask the IRS for Form 4506—Request for Copy of Tax Form.

Lastly, secure all records relating to a specific tax year in an envelope and store it in a safe place.

Penalties for understatement of tax liability. Whenever noncompliance with the tax laws results in an underpayment of tax due to negligence or intentional disregard of rules and regulations, you're subject to a penalty equal to 5% of the amount of the deficiency related to negligence, interest, and an additional penalty equal to 50% of the interest due on the underpayment. Under the provisions of the Tax Reform Act of 1986, the penalty for substantial understatement of tax liability is 25% of the amount of the understatement, and the penalty for any amount attributable to fraud is 75% of the amount of the deficiency related to fraud. Both penalties apply to returns required to be filed on or after January 1, 1987. ■

Medical & Dental Deductions

Medical & Dental Expenses

Medical and dental expenses are any payments or costs related to the diagnosis, cure, relief, mitigation, treatment, or prevention of disease or for the purpose of affecting any part or function of the body. Physical and mental disorders, defects, and illnesses are all diseases.

Payments of this type for you, your spouse, and your dependents are deductible on Schedule A only in the year paid. You must reduce your medical expenses by the amount of any reimbursements received, and effective in 1987, your deduction is limited to the amount of medical and dental expenses that exceeds 7½% (previously 5%) of your adjusted gross income.

Payments for a spouse and dependents. For medical expenses of a spouse to be deductible, you must have been married either at the time your spouse received the medical services or at the time you paid the bills. Similarly, you can deduct your dependents' medical expenses as long as they qualified as a dependent either at the time the expenses were incurred or when you paid them.

Medical expenses for a child of divorced or separated parents are deductible by the person who pays them, regardless of who has custody or who claims the dependency exemption.

Deductible Expenses

The major categories of deductible medical and dental expenses are discussed below. Also be sure to see the checklist that begins on page 19.

Prescription medicines and drugs. Deductible medications include only those that legally require a prescription by a doctor. Insulin is allowable, but no deduction is allowed for any over-the-counter medicines or drugs.

Doctors, dentists, nurses, and hospitals. Amounts paid to individuals and institutions for medical care, along with insurance premiums (discussed later), and payments for psychiatric care are deductible, including care in a specially equipped facility and the cost of doctor-recommended regular visits as part of the patient's treatment.

Deductible dental expenses include dentists' fees, braces, dentures, extractions, fillings, teeth cleaning, and X-rays.

Wages and meals you provide for an attendant who provides nursing-type services are deductible, but you can't deduct for any time the attendant spends on personal or household tasks. Also include any extra expenses you incur because of the attendant, such as extra rent, utilities, and social security or other employment taxes.

Alcohol and drug abuse treatment costs, including meals and lodging at the center during the course of treatment, are deductible as medical expenses. So are transplant expenses, including payments for surgical, hospital, laboratory, and travel expenses of a donor or possible donor.

Hospital expenses include ambulance hire; fees for dental, diagnostic, laboratory, obstetrical, surgical, and X-ray services; therapy; and nursing services.

Automobile and other transportation expenses.

Amounts spent for transportation necessary for medical care are deductible. Such trips may include those related to paying medical insurance premiums and trips to a pharmacy to purchase prescription medicines, as well as away-from-home travel.

Costs of away-from-home medical travel are allowed by the IRS if the trip is primarily for medical purposes, not pleasure or personal interests; if the person taking the trip has a specific ailment or condition and was treated previously by someone in a medical capacity; and if the destination helps alleviate or cure the ailment or condition, is temporary, and was advised by a doctor.

Car expenses, whether local or away from home, are deductible at the current standard mileage rate of 9¢ per mile. Or, you may deduct your actual cost of gas and oil. To determine actual cost, total your gas and oil expenses and divide by the total miles driven during the year; then multiply by your medical mileage. Keep the computation and use this rate if it's more than the standard rate. Parking fees and tolls are fully deductible either way. General repairs and maintenance, insurance, and depreciation are *not* deductible.

Medical-related transportation costs by other vehicles, including bus, plane, train, and ambulance, are also deductible, as are the costs of a nurse or other person who must accompany you or your dependent to receive medical care.

Meals and lodging. Include these expenses on Schedule A with your transportation costs if the meals and lodging are provided by a hospital or similar institution and the main reason for being there is to receive medical care. You can also include the cost of nonhospital lodging while away from home if you meet the following conditions:

1. It's essential and primarily for medical care.
2. A doctor provides medical care in a licensed hospital or similar facility.
3. There's no significant element of personal pleasure associated with the trip.
4. Any lodging provided isn't lavish or extravagant.

You can deduct up to $50 per night for the patient and for each person required to help the patient. Meals and lodging en route are also deductible but *not* after arrival, unless the patient is hospitalized.

Nursing and retirement homes. The entire cost of medical care received in a nursing home or home for the aged for a dependent, spouse, or yourself is deductible if the primary reason for being there is for medical reasons. Your case for deducting the entire cost will be enhanced if a physician ordered or recommended the location.

Medical expenses incurred in retirement homes that set medical costs apart from monthly or lump-sum life-care or founder's fees are deductible if required as a condition for the home's promise to provide lifetime care.

Insurance premiums. Along with your payments to doctors, dentists, and hospitals, deduct the amount of insurance premiums paid for policies that provide for direct payments or reimbursements, regardless of who receives them, to cover medical expenses. Also deduct payments for membership in an association that provides group hospitalization, clinical care, or cooperative or so-called "free-choice" medical services.

If you *voluntarily* pay premiums to obtain Medicare A hospital insurance, these payments are deductible. But Medicare A costs included in mandatory social security taxes withheld from wages (or paid with self-employment tax) for hospital insurance are not deductible.

Premiums for Medicare B, supplementary medical insurance for the aged, are deductible for each month of enrollment.

If you're not yet 65 and prepay premiums for medical care coverage after you reach 65 for yourself, your spouse, or a dependent, they're deductible in the year paid if they're payable either in equal yearly installments or more often. Premiums must be payable for at least 10 years or until you reach age 65 (but in no case for less than 5 years).

Employer health plans that provide continued coverage after you retire allow you to choose between receiving a cash payment for unused sick leave or applying it against future premiums. If you choose the latter, you must include the value of the unused sick leave in your gross income and deduct the applied amount as a medical insurance premium. However, if your plan automatically applies the sick leave value to your premiums, there's no reporting required.

Special medical items and equipment. You can deduct the cost of hand controls or other special auto equipment installed for a physically handicapped person but not the day-to-day operating costs of the car. The purchase price and maintenance costs of an autoette (a small auto for the handicapped) or a wheelchair used primarily for the alleviation of sickness or disability (not simply for transportation to work) are allowable medical expenses. If a car is designed or modified to carry a wheelchair, only the extra cost is deductible.

The costs of guide dogs and their care are deductible, as are the costs of braille books, escorts for the blind, handrails, and special telephone and television equipment for the deaf.

Payments for oxygen and related equipment to relieve breathing problems caused by a medical condition are also deductible.

Special medical care for the handicapped. You can deduct payments for the costs of meals, lodging, and ordinary education supplied by a special school for a mentally or physically handicapped person if the school is used primarily because of its resources for relieving the handicap. Tuition fees and tutoring (if advised by a doctor) by specially trained teachers qualified to deal with severe learning disabilities caused by a nervous system disorder are also deductible.

Capital expenditures. If you install special equipment in your home or make major improvements to it for medical reasons, you may be able to deduct all or part of the cost. Though not required, it's helpful to obtain a statement from a doctor as to why the equipment or improvement was necessary. If the improvement doesn't increase the value of your home, you can deduct the entire amount. If your property increases in value, however, the cost of the improvement is reduced by the increase in value, and any resulting balance is then deducted as a medical expense. Get an appraisal if substantial amounts are involved.

Even if your deduction is reduced or eliminated by the increase in value, you can still deduct the costs of operation and upkeep. Add the undeducted cost of improvements to the adjusted basis of your home.

Handicapped persons who make improvements to rented property on their doctor's advice can deduct their costs if the rent is not lowered due to an increase in value.

Medical or business deduction? Often, an expense can be deductible as either a medical or a business expense. It's usually best to classify it as a business expense, since the limitation on employee business expenses under the Tax Reform Act of 1986 is 2%, as opposed to 7½% for medical expenses. Deduct medical expenses as business expenses only if they meet all the following criteria:

1. They're clearly required for you to do your work satisfactorily.
2. They're for goods and services not ordinarily needed or used in personal activities.
3. The code and regulations don't provide for how the expense should be treated.

An example of such an expense is a person confined to a wheelchair who must be away from home for business purposes and who needs a helper for certain tasks (though the helper is not needed ordinarily). Payments for the helper's travel, meals, and lodging are deductible as a business expense.

Handling Reimbursements

Medical expenses must be reduced by reimbursements received (including those from Medicare) before applying the 7½% limitation. However, how you report (or do not report) these reimbursements depends on several factors, such as when the reimbursement was received and if a deduction was claimed in a prior year. It also depends on who paid the insurance premium. Since this can have a significant effect on your deduction, it's essential to keep careful track of reimbursements.

Accident insurance. Policies of this type usually reimburse you for hospitalization and medical care; you then reduce your expenses by the amounts so designated. You do *not* have to include any reimbursements received for loss of earnings or damages for personal injury.

Personal injury settlement. If you settle a personal injury suit, the payments received are treated the same as insurance reimbursements. If the settlement includes a fixed amount for medical treatment of a specific injury in future years, you must continue to reduce your medical expenses until the amount received has been completely used. Only then can you begin to claim deductions for medical expenses attributable to those injuries. Do not include any unused reimbursements in income, since treatment for the injuries could recur.

Excess reimbursement. How you treat such reimbursements depends on whether you, your employer, or both of you paid the premium.

When *you* pay the entire premium and the reimbursement is equal to or exceeds your expenses, there's no deduction for that claim and you don't include the excess in income or, more importantly, offset it against other medical expenses.

When *your employer* pays the entire premium and such contributions are not included in your income, you must include any excess reimbursements as income and report that income on your return for that year.

17

When you *both* contribute to the cost of your medical plan and your employer's contributions are not included in your gross income, you only use the employer's proportionate part of excess reimbursements to reduce all medical expenses.

Reimbursement received in a later year. When you receive a reimbursement in a later year for medical expenses you deducted in an earlier year, you must do one of the following:

1. Include as income the amount received that is equal to or less than that previously deducted.
2. Exclude from income the amount received up to the amount that did not decrease income subject to tax in the year deducted.

See page 35 for a worksheet that may help you figure any income to be included.

Expenses not deducted in an earlier year. Suppose you had medical expenses in an earlier year that you did not deduct because you didn't itemize, they didn't exceed the limitation, or they were disallowed. Reimbursements received in a later year should not be included in income unless they're greater than the expense, in which case the excess reimbursement rules apply.

When & How to Deduct Medical Expenses

As with other itemized deductions, you claim the deduction in the year of actual payment, after subtracting any reimbursements. Once the amounts are entered on Schedule A, you total all categories and subtract an amount equal to 7½% of your adjusted gross income. This will give you your total allowable medical expense deduction for the year.

Spouses filing separate returns can each deduct only the medical expenses separately paid. If payments for medical expenses are made from the couple's joint checking account, each is considered to have made half the payment, unless shown otherwise.

Tax$aver Tip. *Consider filing separate returns when you have large medical bills. Try to project what the adjusted gross income and tax bracket will be for each spouse; then pay the bills from the separate account of the spouse who will benefit the most from the deduction.*

Medical Expense Deduction Checklist

The following is a checklist of the types of deductible and nondeductible payments related to medical or dental care. If an expense is unusual or especially large, it's advisable to obtain a written statement from your physician recommending it. Any medical costs incurred to improve your health in a general way, as opposed to being for a specific disease or condition, are generally not deductible, even when advised by your doctor.

Note that deductible expenses mentioned in the text are not repeated in the checklist.

Checklist of Deductible Medical & Dental Expenses

Abortion

Acupuncturist, chiropractor, midwife fees

Ambulance service

Artificial limbs, support or corrective devices

Blood transfusions, laboratory and X-ray fees

Checkups, medical and dental

Contact lenses

Contraceptive devices and products, sterilization

Cosmetic and plastic surgery*, collagen shots

Credit card charges for medical expenses

Diets and weight loss programs related to a specific ailment*

Electrolysis or hair removal

Eye exams, eyeglasses

Fluoride device (including rental fees) added to home water supply

Foreign travel if treatment not available in U.S.

Hearing aids, sign-language and lipreading lessons, hired companions for deaf

Hospice services

Hypodermic needles, medical injections

Instruction and training for blind or deaf

Insurance premiums paid for accident and disability, auto and homeowner's medical coverage (if separately stated), contact lens replacement, employer health plans for retirees, group medical and clinical plans, health maintenance organizations, hospitalization and surgery, Medicare A if paid voluntarily, Medicare B, prescription drugs

Journals and magazines about specific disorders

Legal fees for mental illness treatment

Massage if prescribed and therapeutic

Rental and repair of medical equipment

19

Special home for mentally retarded dependent

Wigs and hairpieces advised by doctor

*Subject to certain rules and restrictions

Checklist of Nondeductible Medical Expenses

Aerobic exercises; golf, tennis, dancing, and swimming lessons

Dues to health clubs, YMCA, YWCA

Funeral and burial expenses

Household help (nonmedical)

Insurance policy premiums for auto medical coverage (other than family) for persons injured in or by your car; life insurance; payments for loss of earnings, loss of life, etc.

Marriage counseling, seminar

Meals and lodging away from home for treatment at nonmedical facility

Nursing services for normal, healthy baby

Relative's home used for mentally retarded person

Stop-smoking programs

Toiletries, cosmetics, bottled or distilled water

Travel to and from work even if unusual due to health conditions

Vacation trip recommended for change in environment or morale

Vacuum cleaner to alleviate dust in air

Using the Medical & Dental Expense Forms

Under the 7½% limitation, only major medical expenses are going to be allowed as a deduction. Keeping track of such expenses and determining which ones are reimbursable and by whom can be a real headache. Whatever your family medical situation, using the forms that follow can help ease your burden. Be sure to keep all bills.

Medical & Dental Expense Register. Make entries in this register as they occur, and if applicable, bill Medicare or your insurance company promptly. Every time you make a payment, record it along with the invoice information. Record any reimbursements as they're received.

Tax$aver Tip. *When you've paid the premium, it's important to match each reimbursement with the appropriate*

expense claim. When the reimbursement is less than the amount claimed, enter the net expense. But the rules say that when the reimbursement exceeds your claim, you can enter zero. Thus, the excess is not offset against other medical expenses, giving you a larger deduction.

This benefit is not available if your employer paid the premium.

The total of each column labeled "Net Deductible Expense" can be entered directly on Schedule A. Keep all records in a large envelope and store with this book.

Record of Medical Expenses Reimbursable from Others. Many medical expenses covered by Medicare or a health insurance plan have to be paid by you first and then submitted for reimbursement. Other bills can be submitted when received, in which case either you receive a check or the bill is paid directly to the doctor or hospital. It's very important to be informed and up to date on the status of any one bill at all times.

If you must pay the bill first, enter your check number to establish that the bill was paid. If the payment is billable to others, note to whom, and record the date it's sent in for payment plus the amount you're seeking. When the payment is received, enter the date and amount on the same line as it was billed. Often, certain types of expenses aren't covered under Medicare. Enter the amount and reason for these disallowances; sometimes, these amounts can be billed to your insurance company, so review your policy. Record these billings in the same manner as for Medicare.

This record is also the source of entries you make in the Medical & Dental Expense Register in the insurance reimbursements columns.

Log of Deductible Travel for Medical & Dental Purposes. Use this log to record both local and away-from-home travel expenses for medical purposes. At year end, enter the total from the "Net Deductible Expense" column directly on Schedule A on the line provided for transportation and lodging. ■

Medical & Dental Expense Register

Date 19 __	Paid to/Date of Invoice/For Whom Nature & Purpose of Service Rendered	Ck. #, Cr. Card, or Cash	Prescription Medicines & Drugs			Medical Care		
			Cost	Less Insurance Reimb.	Net Deductible Expense	Doctors	Dentists	Hospitals
				( )				
				( )				
				( )				
				( )				
				( )				
				( )				
				( )				
				( )				
				( )				
				( )				
				( )				
				( )				
				( )				
				( )				
				( )				
	Subtotals			( )				

Medical Care (Continued)						Other Medical Items			
Insurance Premiums	Other Medical		Total Medical Care	Less Insurance Reimb.	Net Deductible Expense	Description	Amount	Less Insurance Reimb.	Net Deductible Expense
	Description	Amount							
				( )				( )	
				( )				( )	
				( )				( )	
				( )				( )	
				( )				( )	
				( )				( )	
				( )				( )	
				( )				( )	
				( )				( )	
				( )				( )	
				( )				( )	
				( )				( )	
				( )				( )	
				( )				( )	
				( )				( )	
				( )				( )	

Medical & Dental Expense Register

Date 19 __ / Paid to/Date of Invoice/For Whom / Nature & Purpose of Service Rendered	Ck. #, Cr. Card, or Cash	Prescription Medicines & Drugs			Medical Care		
		Cost	Less Insurance Reimb.	Net Deductible Expense	Doctors	Dentists	Hospitals
			( )				
			( )				
			( )				
			( )				
			( )				
			( )				
			( )				
			( )				
			( )				
			( )				
			( )				
			( )				
			( )				
			( )				
			( )				
			( )				
Note: Transfer totals directly to Schedule A.	Totals for Year		( )				

Medical Care (Continued)						Other Medical Items			
Insurance Premiums	Other Medical		Total Medical Care	Less Insurance Reimb.	Net Deductible Expense	Description	Amount	Less Insurance Reimb.	Net Deductible Expense
	Description	Amount							
				( )				( )	
				( )				( )	
				( )				( )	
				( )				( )	
				( )				( )	
				( )				( )	
				( )				( )	
				( )				( )	
				( )				( )	
				( )				( )	
				( )				( )	
				( )				( )	
				( )				( )	
				( )				( )	
				( )				( )	
				( )				( )	

Record of Medical Expenses Reimbursable from Others

Date of Visit	Doctor, Hospital, or Clinic	Type of Treatment	Length of Visit	Total Fee		If Paid, Check #	To Be Billed	
							Medi-care	Insur-ance Co.
1/10/87	Dr. L. Brown	Chest X ray	30 min.	80	00	238	✓	✓

Billed & Due from Medicare						Billed & Due from Insurance Co. or Others					
Billed		Payments Rec'd.		Fees Disallowed		Billed		Payments Rec'd.		Fees Disallowed	
Date	Amount	Date	Amount	Amount	Reason	Date	Amount	Date	Amount	Amount	Reason
2/2	80 00	3/5	56 00	24 00	approved #70 Paid 80%	3/8	24 00	3/22	14 00	10 00	not approved by Medicare

Record of Medical Expenses Reimbursable from Others

Date of Visit	Doctor, Hospital, or Clinic	Type of Treatment	Length of Visit	Total Fee		If Paid, Check #	To Be Billed	
							Medi-care	Insur-ance Co.

Billed & Due from Medicare						Billed & Due from Insurance Co. or Others					
Billed		Payments Rec'd.		Fees Disallowed		Billed		Payments Rec'd.		Fees Disallowed	
Date	Amount	Date	Amount	Amount	Reason	Date	Amount	Date	Amount	Amount	Reason

Log of Deductible Travel for Medical & Dental Purposes

Date 19 __	Destination & Reason for Trip / Mode of Transportation	Standard Mileage Rate Method					Actual Cost Method	Parking Fees & Tolls	Meals & Lodging	Total Expenses	Less Reimb.		Net Deduct. Expense
		Odometer		Computation									
		Start	End	Miles	Rate	Cost	Gas & Oil						
					× 9¢						(	)	
					× 9¢						(	)	
					× 9¢						(	)	
					× 9¢						(	)	
					× 9¢						(	)	
					× 9¢						(	)	
					× 9¢						(	)	
					× 9¢						(	)	
					× 9¢						(	)	
					× 9¢						(	)	
					× 9¢						(	)	
					× 9¢						(	)	
					× 9¢						(	)	
					× 9¢						(	)	
					× 9¢						(	)	
					× 9¢						(	)	

Log of Deductible Travel for Medical & Dental Purposes

Date 19 __	Destination & Reason for Trip / Mode of Transportation	Standard Mileage Rate Method						Actual Cost Method	Parking Fees & Tolls	Meals & Lodging	Total Expenses	Less Reimb.		Net Deduct. Expense
		Odometer		Computation				Gas & Oil						
		Start	End	Miles	Rate	Cost								
					× 9¢							(	)	
					× 9¢							(	)	
					× 9¢							(	)	
					× 9¢							(	)	
					× 9¢							(	)	
					× 9¢							(	)	
					× 9¢							(	)	
					× 9¢							(	)	
					× 9¢							(	)	
					× 9¢							(	)	
					× 9¢							(	)	
					× 9¢							(	)	
					× 9¢							(	)	
					× 9¢							(	)	
					× 9¢							(	)	
Note: Transfer totals directly to Schedule A.	**Totals for Year**				× 9¢							(	)	

Taxes

Present tax law allows individuals to claim the following tax payments as itemized deductions:

1. Income taxes—state, local, and foreign
2. Real estate taxes—state, local, and foreign
3. Personal property taxes—state and local

In order to be deductible, the tax must be imposed on you and must actually be paid during the tax year. For a checklist of deductible and non-deductible tax payments, see page 40.

Beginning in 1987, state and local sales taxes are no longer deductible under the Tax Reform Act of 1986. If paid for property used in a business or investment activity, sales tax must be treated as part of the cost of acquiring property (subject to depreciation) or as a reduction in the amount realized when disposition occurs.

State, Local & Foreign Income Taxes

Payments for income, war profits, and excess profits taxes are deductible if paid to the following:

1. The District of Columbia, any of the states that collect state income tax, or U.S. possessions
2. Any of their political subdivisions, such as a city or county
3. Foreign countries or any of their political subdivisions

These taxes are deductible even if they're not related to a trade or business or production of income/investment activity. However, foreign income taxes are not deductible if the foreign earned-income exclusion applies or if the foreign tax credit is claimed against your federal income tax liability. This deduction or credit arising from an investment in a foreign company is allowed so that taxpayers can avoid having the income taxed by both the foreign country and the U.S.

If you're an employee and mandatory amounts are withheld from your wages and contributed to a state nonoccupational or temporary disability fund, they're deductible as state income taxes.

Determining your deduction. Your total deduction for state, local, and foreign income taxes can be derived from various sources. Here's what it could include:

1. Amounts withheld from your wages during the year per your W-2 forms
2. Estimated tax payments actually paid during the year, whether for the prior or current year
3. A credit for overpayment in a previous year which is not refunded but which instead is applied as an estimated tax payment for the following year (show the overpayment as a refund on Form 1040 and include the same amount with your other payments on Schedule A)
4. Amounts due for the immediately preceding year but paid in the current year
5. Amounts due for next year but paid before December 31, as long as the basis for the estimation is reasonable
6. Any additional tax paid in the current year which is for any prior year due to an audit adjustment or from filing an amended return

Refunds of state, local, and foreign income taxes. A taxpayer may receive an income tax refund due to an amended return, an audit, a mathematical error, or the overwithholding of tax. When your refund is over $10, both you and the IRS will receive Form 1099-G, which will allow the IRS to check that you've included the refund on your return.

If you receive a refund in the current year for an overpayment of state income tax in a prior year and you did *not* itemize your deductions that year, *none* of your refund is included in income in the current year—it's tax free. However, any interest received on the refund would be taxable. Because the IRS receives Form 1099-G, you should attach a note to your return stating the amount of the refund and that it's not included because you did not itemize in the prior year. Otherwise, it could trigger an audit.

If you did itemize in the prior year and your excess itemized deductions were greater than the amount of the state tax refund received, you must include *all* of the refund on the appropriate line on Form 1040 for the current year.

However, if your excess itemized deductions were less than the amount of the refund you received, use the following IRS worksheet to figure out how much of your refund should be included in taxable income on Form 1040:

1. Enter the income tax refund from Form 1099-G or similar statement $ _____

2. Enter the amount of excess itemized deductions from the prior year's Schedule A $ _____

3. Compare the amounts above and enter the lesser amount here and on Form 1040 on the refund line $ _____

If any of the conditions below apply to a refund you received in the current year for a prior tax year, either refer to IRS Publication 525 or ask your tax advisor to determine the amount to be included in income.

- Your zero bracket amount was more than your taxable income for that year.

- You had a negative taxable income that year.

- You received a refund other than an income tax refund in the current year of an amount you deducted (or credit you claimed) in an earlier year.

- Your refunds were more than your excess itemized deductions for the year *and* included a state or local income tax refund.

Taking the deduction. State and local income taxes deducted by married couples are subject to certain rules. When a joint return is filed, it doesn't matter that one spouse pays the other's taxes or expenses—they're always deductible.

However, when married couples file separate state and federal returns, each spouse can deduct on their federal return only the state income taxes each actually paid. More importantly, if one spouse pays the other's tax, *neither* can deduct it.

Tax$aver Tip. *Eliminate this possibility by maintaining separate bank accounts; have one spouse loan funds to the other, if necessary, so as not to lose the deduction.*

If spouses file separate state returns but file jointly for federal purposes, the deduction for the joint return is the sum of the state income taxes imposed and paid by both. It's irrelevant who actually paid the taxes.

Finally, when a joint state return is filed and federal returns are filed separately, each can deduct on their federal returns only state income taxes imposed and paid based on their own gross income, but only in states where one spouse isn't liable for the other's taxes. If all or a portion is paid by the other spouse, *neither* gets a deduction.

> **Tax$aver Tip.** *There's a valuable tax-saving exception in states where both spouses are jointly and severally liable for the full amount of state income taxes imposed and they file separate federal returns. Each spouse can deduct the total amount they actually paid, regardless of whom the tax was imposed on. Thus, when you can plan to file separate federal returns, the spouse in the highest tax bracket should pay the tax and claim the deduction to achieve the maximum tax savings.*

If you live in a community property state and you and your spouse file separate returns, half the deductible expenses paid from funds you both own are considered as paid by each of you. But if paid from separate funds, only the spouse paying the expense is entitled to the deduction.

Real Estate Taxes

To be deductible, real property taxes must be levied by proper taxing authorities (state, local, or foreign) at a like rate against all property in the territory over which such authorities have jurisdiction and must be for the welfare of the general public. The tax must be imposed on *you*, and *you* must be legally obligated for its payment.

There's an exception when another person has legal title (such as a tenant in common) and is assessed the tax and you own a beneficial interest in the property. If you pay the tax to protect your interest, the payment is deductible. Similarly, if there is more than one owner and all are equally responsible, the one who pays the entire tax may deduct the entire amount. Shareholders in a cooperative housing corporation who are also tenants can deduct their share of the corporation's real estate taxes, as can owners of a condominium used as a principal residence.

The majority of homeowners or property owners make monthly payments that include an estimate for real estate taxes and insurance due in the near future. These monies are placed in an escrow account and accumulate until the date payments must be made. However, your deduction is based only on the amounts actually paid to the taxing authority. They or the lender will usually send you information at the end of the year as to the total paid during the year.

Other real property taxes. Special assessments and so-called local benefit taxes that tend to increase the value and benefit specific properties are not deductible. Typical examples are construction and improvements for local streets, sidewalks, public parking facilities, and the like.

However, taxes assessed against local benefits *are* deductible if they are paid for the purpose of meeting repairs or maintenance costs or interest charges related to the local benefit. But the burden of proof as to how the allocation between deductible and nondeductible expenses was made rests with the taxpayer. Even if some portion known to be local benefits is included in the taxes paid, no portion is deductible if no allocation can be made. Consult your taxing authority.

Taking the deduction. Real estate taxes, with few exceptions, are generally deducted by the assessed owner of the property or the person otherwise legally obligated for the payment. One exception is when real estate is sold and an allocation has to be made between buyer and seller according to the number of days each owned the property, regardless of any contract between the parties, whom the tax is imposed on, or who pays it. When one spouse owns a home and pays the real estate taxes, they can be deducted either on that spouse's separate return or on the couple's joint return.

When property is held as tenants by the entirety or as joint property and separate returns are filed, each spouse can deduct only the taxes that each paid. Tenants in common can deduct their pro rata share of property taxes if each has reimbursement rights from the other for taxes paid.

Tax$aver Tip. *Any taxes you pay that are not deductible because of allocation rules or*

*for any other reason can be treated as a
sale expense or added to basis. When the
property is sold, these additions to basis
will either reduce the gain on the sale or
increase any loss.*

Personal Property Taxes

State and local personal property taxes are
deductible by the property owner only if *all* of
the following requirements are satisfied:

1. The assessed tax must be an ad valorem tax,
   which means assessed in proportion to the
   value of the property.
2. It must be imposed on an annual basis, no
   matter how frequently it's collected.
3. It must be imposed on personal property or
   for the exercise of a privilege, such as using a
   vehicle on the highways.

Approximately one-third of the states have
allowable tax deductions of this type. Depending
on where you live, all or part of such a tax may
be deductible. If a state bases its tax on weight,
model year, horsepower, or any characteristic

other than value, it's not an ad valorem tax and is
not deductible. However, a tax based partly on
value and partly on other criteria, like weight, is
deductible only as to the value portion of the tax.
Because rates and fees can change, consult your
local taxing authority.

Taking the deduction. Personal property taxes are
generally deductible only by the owner of the
property. An exception could be a requirement
under an automobile lease agreement for the
lessee to pay annual registration fees, which, if
based on the value of the car, are deductible.

Claiming Your Deductions

Income, real estate, and personal property taxes
are all deducted on Schedule A.

When to deduct tax payments. For a tax to be
deductible, it must actually be paid during the
tax year. For virtually all cash basis taxpayers, this
means the calendar year, January through
December. It doesn't matter if the tax is related
to any prior, current, or future tax year.

If you pay by cash, *always* get a dated receipt—it's the only way you can prove the time of payment. If you pay by check, the date of payment is considered to be the day you personally deliver the check to the payee or when it's mailed.

Tax$aver Tip. *If you're paying a large deductible amount or it's subject to penalties, make sure your letter is postmarked by the applicable due date. An alternative is to certify or register it with the post office; or ask the payee to write to you confirming the postmark date and date received.*

Some institutions allow payments to be made over the phone either by credit card or by transfer of funds. In this case, the payment date is the date reported on the institution's statement to you. When calling in the payment, ask when it will be recorded on their records as a payment and take whatever action is necessary to secure the deduction.

Payments by credit card are now treated as cash payments on the date charged, even though payment to the credit card company might occur in the following tax year.

An entirely different situation exists when you contest a certain tax liability and pay it under protest. It's still deductible in the year of payment, but if settled later for a lesser amount, the refund must be included in income in the year received.

Proving your deductions. In the event of an audit by the IRS, you'll need to show how you arrived at the total deduction amount for each category of expense claimed. The expense register following this section is designed to help you record and accumulate all your tax payments by category. To prove that the payment was incurred for the purpose specified, you'll need documents, receipts, canceled checks, or other evidence.

You can document your deduction for state and local income taxes with employers' W-2 statements. Other evidence includes copies of estimated tax declarations and tax returns showing overpayments credited against estimated tax or amounts due when the return was filed.

Real estate tax payments can be documented by receipted, dated tax bills or statements sent to you by your lender or taxing authority. Monthly statements from the lender may show additions to the escrow account and also reductions to the account when payment is made. For allocated taxes between buyer and seller, each should receive a closing or settlement statement.

For most personal property tax payments, you'll receive a registration or license document which, together with the canceled check, should verify the amount paid.

Taxes Checklist

The following checklist for deductible and nondeductible taxes relates only to Schedule A. Taxes mentioned in the text are not repeated here.

Deductible Taxes

Related to State, Local, or Foreign Income Taxes

Tax paid on interest income exempt from federal income tax

Unemployment fund contributions required by state law to provide against lost wages

Related to Real Estate Taxes (State, Local, or Foreign)

Assessment for retirement of an old bond issue for a resident of community benefited

Condominium owner's proportionate share of real estate taxes on owner's own unit plus tax on common areas of the building and grounds

Local assessments on essential or special services, such as police and fire protection, street cleaning, and lighting only if imposed at a uniform rate on users and all owners of designated properties

Tax paid by a lessee who was allowed by local law to be entered on tax assessment roll

Tax paid on a condominium in a foreign country, even though owner is not allowed legal title

Tax paid on donated property where donor retained right to use property

Tax paid on a residence solely owned by one spouse where ex-spouse occupied it rent-free

Tax paid on vacant, unimproved, or raw land whether held for investment or not

Related to Personal Property Taxes

Amounts allowable as a deduction for motor vehicles, even when standard mileage rate method is used to deduct business mileage

Registration or licensing fee for any portion of a tax based on value of cars, trucks, motorcycles, motor homes, mobile homes, house and travel trailers, boats, and airplanes

Related to Production of Income

State and local transfer taxes on sale of stocks and bonds

State, local, and foreign taxes of any kind incurred in order to produce income

Related to Miscellaneous Taxes

Credit card charges for any type of deductible tax on date charged, not when paid

Installment payments on any otherwise deductible tax in year paid

Involuntary, mandatory extractions from salaries or wages by a state for any kind of tax

Nondeductible Taxes

Related to Federal, State, or Local Income Taxes

Federal income taxes or surtax paid or withheld

Federal unemployment taxes

Federal war and excess profits taxes

Income tax withheld on nonresident aliens and tax-free covenant bonds

Personal holding company tax

State or local income tax paid on income (other than interest income) exempt from federal income tax

Tax (federal) on self-employment income

Tax on transfers to avoid income taxes

Related to Real Estate Taxes

Assessments by homeowners' associations for maintenance of common areas and recreational facilities

Assessments for water bills, sewer user fees, trash collection, and other service charges*

Delinquent taxes paid by buyer of real property as part of contract price, even when imposed on seller (can be added to basis)

Escrow amounts included in monthly payments for real property taxes

Penalties on delinquent real property taxes

Real property taxes imposed on another but paid by taxpayer, even if under court order

Sanitation service fee collected with real property tax*

41

Shareholder's (in cooperative housing
corporation) portion of real estate taxes when
corporation leases land and buildings and
must pay real estate taxes per lease agreement*
Taxes paid by guarantor on foreclosed property

Related to Personal Property Taxes
License plates, personalized or not*
Motor vehicle taxes and registration fees*

Related to Other Federal, State, or Local Taxes
Excise taxes if imposed on private foundations,
qualified pension plans, real estate investment
trusts, or public charities on excess expendi-
tures to influence legislation
Estate, gift, inheritance, legacy, succession, per
capita, or poll tax
Federal excise taxes on air transportation,
gasoline, tires, etc.*
Filing fees for candidates in primary elections
Fines for parking, speeding, or other violations
Gasoline, diesel, and other motor fuel taxes*
Penalties for failing to file a return (even if
assessed as a tax) or for violation of any law

Renters' tax imposed on tenants as a percentage
of monthly rent*
Social Security or railroad retirement taxes
Taxes on admission, alcoholic beverages,
cigarettes, occupancy, tobacco*
Telephone and teletype service excise taxes*
Title registration fees
Transfer taxes on stock or securities given to a
relative or charity

Related to Foreign Taxes
Personal property, sales, and gasoline taxes*
Taxes of foreign countries or U.S. possessions
if foreign tax credit is elected

Related to Miscellaneous Taxes
Any charge that's a fee for services*
Employee voluntary contributions to any
disability plans
Municipal utilities district charges*
Old-age benefit contributions by employees
Payments to nongovernmental organizations,
even when used for same purposes as taxes*

*May be deductible if related to trade, business,

or income-producing activity or under certain other circumstances

Using the Tax Expense Register

Use the register to record all deductible tax payments in one convenient place, regardless of how paid, and in the same categories that appear on Schedule A. On a periodic basis, record all your tax payments as they occur during the year. Stay up to date—at the end of the year, you'll only have to record the most recent transactions in order to total the register and transfer the amounts directly to Schedule A.

Always indicate whether a receipt was obtained and staple it to the canceled check or credit card slip.

Tax$aver Tip. *When you're due a tax refund and you've kept track of withheld taxes on a periodic basis, double-check with your employer to see if your totals are correct for the year and prepare your return. Then,*

when you get your W-2, you can just attach a copy and file the return immediately. This way, you'll receive your refund more quickly.

Enter overpayments applied against declarations of estimated tax from your prior year's return or attach copies of the filed declaration forms.

For tax payments that are not deducted but are added to the cost basis of property you own, you'll need to retain this book for at least 3 years after you sell the property in order to properly document these additions. ■

Tax Expense Register

Date 19__	Paid to/Description	Ck. #, Cash, or Cr. Card	Receipt Yes	Receipt No	Income Taxes State, Local, or Foreign	Income Taxes Estimated Tax Paid	Income Taxes Withheld from Wages	Income Taxes Overpayment or Credit	Income Taxes Other Payments
Note: Enter one total monthly or quarterly for income taxes withheld from wages.		**Totals for Year**							

Real Estate Taxes				Personal Property Taxes	Other Taxes Paid			Added to Basis	
Paid Directly by You	Paid by Others for You	Allocated to You due to Sale	Added to Basis of Property					Description	Amount

Interest

Interest is any expense you pay for the use of borrowed money. In the past, nonbusiness and investment interest payments were generally fully deductible on Schedule A. However, the Tax Reform Act of 1986 has significantly affected the deductibility of interest payments, as explained on the following pages.

To be deductible, your interest payments must be due to an existing, valid, and enforceable obligation resulting from a true debtor-creditor relationship and must be paid by you during the tax year. Any amount specified in the loan agreement that can be definitely determined as the cost of borrowed money may be deductible, even if the percentage rate is not stated.

Home Mortgage Interest

For most taxpayers, mortgage interest is the largest interest expense item claimed, since the majority of the monthly payment on a home mortgage is attributable to interest.

Under the Tax Reform Act of 1986, interest on mortgages secured either by your principal residence or a second home is deductible *only* if the loans are not greater than the original purchase price plus the cost of any improvements you've made to the property. If the loans exceed this amount, the interest is still deductible to the extent the money is used for improvements to the property or for educational or medical purposes. Since special rules apply to particular situations, consult your tax advisor.

Tax$aver Tip. *If you have sufficient equity in your home, you can either get a secured line of credit or refinance, subject to the above limitations, and use the money to pay off consumer loans, since the interest deductions for them are being phased out, starting in 1987.*

Determining your interest payment. To determine the amount of your annual mortgage interest payment, you can use the monthly statements some lending institutions send borrowers showing how the payment is allocated among principal, interest, and real estate taxes. Or use Form 1098—Mortgage Interest Statement, sent to you by January 31 if you paid $600 or more during the previous year. The amount on the statement does not include points or other prepaid interest.

Deducting points. Points is a term used to describe such charges as loan origination fees, maximum loan charges, or premium charges, and basically amounts to an adjustment of the stated interest rate earned at the beginning of the loan. Points can be deducted as interest only if the charge is for the *use* of money, not for a specific service, such as preparing loan documents. In most cases, points are treated like prepaid interest and are deducted pro rata over the term of the mortgage.

However, there's a key exception to this rule that applies to many taxpayers. If the following conditions are met, you can deduct the entire amount paid as points in the year of payment:

1. Your loan is to buy or improve your principal residence and is secured by that residence.
2. The payment of points is an established business practice in the area.
3. The points paid are generally the same as charged by others in the area.
4. The points are actually paid, not just deducted from the loan proceeds.

If you refinance your loan to take advantage of lower interest rates, the points must be deducted over the life of the loan, not in the year the loan is made. When the seller of the property pays points to the lender as a loan placement fee for arranging financing for the buyer, they are not deductible.

Tax$aver Tip. *To secure your deduction for points, ask the financial institution to clearly state the amount of points related to the use of money.*

Cooperatives. If you're a tenant-shareholder in a cooperative housing corporation, you can deduct your proportionate share of points paid by the cooperative in the year you become a tenant-shareholder. Likewise, you can deduct your share of interest on the cooperative's debt in subsequent years. However, the deductions are allowed only if 80% or more of the income of the cooperative housing corporation comes from its tenants.

Owners of units in a condominium can also deduct their proper share of interest and points attributable to their ownership.

Graduated payment mortgages. Such mortgages provide for monthly payments that increase annually for a fixed number of years and then remain the same thereafter. In the early years, the payments are even less than the interest owed, so the unpaid interest is simply added to the loan balance and is not deductible until actually paid.

Shared appreciation mortgages. In this type of mortgage, the lender allows you to pay a lower rate of fixed interest than the prevailing one. In return, the lender gets a contingent interest by sharing in any appreciation in the value of the mortgaged property (usually a specified percentage of the appreciation). This amount is deductible as interest when paid to the lender.

Tax$aver Tip. *If you're refinancing a gradu-ated payment or shared appreciation mortgage, do it with a different lender so you can deduct the interest that's due.*

Reverse mortgage loans. When a lending institution pays you a loan in installments over a period of months or years, it's called a reverse mortgage loan. The loan, secured by a mortgage on your home, is based on its value. When the loan agreement provides that interest is to be added to the loan balance monthly, it's not deductible since you didn't actually pay it.

Other mortgage interest deductions. Your deduction can also include charges for late payments, as long as the charges weren't for a specific service. Despite the general rule that penalties are not deductible, the IRS does allow you to deduct as interest any prepayment penalties charged by the lender for paying off a loan early. And when you sell your home, you can deduct interest up to, but not including, the date of sale.

49

Installment, Credit Card & Charge Account Interest

Consumer interest, such as finance charges paid on retail installment contracts, bank credit cards, oil company credit cards, and revolving charge accounts, are no longer fully deductible under the Tax Reform Act of 1986. In 1987, only 65% of such interest is deductible; in 1988, only 40%; in 1989, only 20%; and in 1990, only 10%. Beginning in 1991, *no* deduction is allowed.

The rule is that consumer interest can be deducted, subject to the above limitations, if separately stated or if able to be determined and proven. Lenders are generally required to express interest and finance charges as an annual percentage rate (APR) on customer billing statements. Such charges are deductible as payments are made over the life of the contract.

Also deductible as interest are original acquisition charges and any fee charged for the privilege of prepaying the contract. The one-time charges added to your credit card balance by the bank for each cash, check, or overdraft advance are deductible as well.

Determining your deduction. Credit card and revolving accounts usually show the interest or finance charge on each month's activity statement; all you have to do is add up all the charges you paid during the year. For retail installment contracts that exceed a year, request a statement from the lender about how much of the total interest or finance charge was allocated to the current tax year.

The rule of 78's method. When interest is added to the principal loan balance and equal payments are made over the life of the loan, your interest deduction each year is claimed on a pro rata or straight-line basis. But different rules apply when the lender requires that for purposes of computing rebates due to early repayment of the loan, the so-called rule of 78's method must be used to allocate payments between principal and interest. This method, favorable to lenders, allows the lender to earn as much income as possible early in the life of the loan.

This provision works to your advantage only if you don't pay off the loan early—you get larger deductions in the early part of the loan and lower deductions later on.

> **Tax$aver Tip.** *With the phase-out of consumer interest deductions, it may not be worth paying off the loan early if very little interest is included in the unpaid balance. Ask the lender for the amounts before deciding.*

The IRS accepts this rule only for loans that qualify as short-term consumer loans. The term must be for no more than 5 years, with no balloon payment at the end, and level payments are required at regular intervals (at least annually). The payments must reduce the loan balance to zero.

Unstated or Imputed Interest

When a sales contract or an installment or other deferred payment plan makes no provision for the payment of interest or provides for a very low rate, it's usually because the seller of the property wants to avoid paying tax on the interest income. Of course, the buyer wants interest included in order to get the deduction.

The IRS, reacting to this problem, enacted regulations requiring that minimum interest rates be charged and paid on such obligations. Under the rules, if the minimum requirements aren't met, interest income is imputed (attributed) to the seller and deductible by the buyer.

Since the rules are complex, it's best to avoid this situation completely. Try to compromise on an interest rate that equals or exceeds the IRS minimum, but is less than can be obtained elsewhere. For more information on unstated interest rules, consult your tax advisor.

Below-Market Interest Rate Loans

Below-market interest rate loans bear either an interest rate less than the applicable federal rate or no interest at all. The code establishes rules which apply to all term loans made after June 6, 1984, and to demand loans (those payable in full at any time upon the lender's demand) outstanding after that date.

Loans subject to these rules include gift loans, corporation-shareholder loans, compensation loans between employee and employer or between independent contractor and client, and tax-avoidance loans. For more information, ask for IRS Publication 545 or see your tax advisor.

Investment Interest

Investors can deduct interest expenses related to loans used to acquire investment property, subject to limitations. The indebtedness generally must be for property that produces taxable income.

Limitations on the amount of investment interest noncorporate taxpayers can deduct have been changed by the Tax Reform Act of 1986. The general rule is that investment interest expense is deductible up to the amount of your net investment income. Formerly, you could deduct an amount equal to your net investment income *plus* $10,000.

The $10,000 allowance is being phased out over 4 years. Therefore, in 1987, investment interest is deductible to the extent of net investment income plus $6,500; in 1988, plus $4,000; in 1989, plus $2,000; and in 1990, plus $1,000. Beginning in 1991, your deduction is limited to net investment income only. Any interest

disallowed may be carried over indefinitely and deducted to the extent of future net investment income.

You'll need careful tax planning to compensate for these mostly adverse changes; discuss your options with your tax advisor.

Other Matters Related to Interest

Here's a brief look at several other points related to your interest deduction.

- When you obtain a loan and use the proceeds to purchase tax-exempt securities, you cannot deduct the interest paid. But if a loan allows you to continue to own those securities as opposed to selling them for needed cash, the interest is deductible if the primary reason for the loan is to use the money for other purposes, not for keeping the securities.
- Generally, unless the loan agreement says otherwise, interim partial payments on a debt are first applied to interest, then to principal.
- When a lump-sum compromise is made for payment of a tax deficiency, penalties, and interest, the interest is deductible when paid as long as a specific amount is allocated as interest. If you make a partial payment and

don't specify how the payment is to be applied, the IRS will apply it in this order—tax, penalty, and interest. The interest portion is subject to the consumer interest limitations.

Tax$aver Tip. *If the above applies to you, be sure to specify that all payments are for interest due until that entire amount has been paid.*

- If you endorse a promissory note of a corporation that is later unable to pay it and you are forced to pay the note and the interest, the interest is deductible, but may be subject to the investment interest limitation.

- When you prematurely withdraw money from a time savings account, you're often charged a penalty. This is deductible (whether you itemize or not), but not as interest expense on Schedule A. Instead, claim it as an adjustment to income on Form 1040.

- You cannot deduct prepaid interest that's not a charge for the use of borrowed money in the current year. Except for points, it must be deducted in the tax year to which it applies.

Refunds of Interest Paid

Cash basis taxpayers who receive a refund of interest in the same year the interest was paid simply report the refund as income on Form 1040 and deduct the interest in full on Schedule A.

But if the refund received was for interest paid in a prior year, you may exclude it entirely if it relates to a year in which you didn't itemize. If you did itemize that year, all or part of it may be income, depending on how much of a tax benefit you received from the payment. If the refund applies to the immediately preceding tax year, use the worksheet on page 35 to do the calculation and attach a copy to your return. If the refund applies to an earlier year, refer to IRS Publication 525 or see your tax advisor.

Interest Expense Checklist

The following list summarizes deductible and nondeductible interest payments, some of which must be spread out over the life of the loan, on various types of personal indebtedness. Refer to it before finalizing your deductions. Deductions

discussed in the text are not repeated here.
Remember that interest deductions on consumer loans must be reduced, starting in 1987.

Deductible Interest

Advance premium payment to get a loan*
Allocated interest from a partnership or S
　corporation*
Charges based on a percentage of unpaid balance
Charges for privilege of deferring payment
Cosigner's interest paid if jointly liable for debt
Debt to acquire ownership in a business
Debt to pay delinquent income taxes
Discount on a note
Family-member loans if bona fide obligation exists*
Ground rents if redeemable*
Insurance policy loans*
Interest paid on another's loan when secured by
　your collateral
Interest related to systematic insurance debt*
IRS interest payments, federal gift tax deficiency
Judgment—interest paid on principal
Loan acquisition or origination fees (but not FHA
　or VA loans)
Margin accounts if paid or available to broker

Nonrecourse financing for tax shelter investments*
Payments in lieu of interest*
Public utility late payment charge if not for
　specific service
Short sale positions after July 18, 1984, for
　payments made to lender in lieu of dividends
Student loans if interest is actually paid

*Deductible subject to certain rules

Nondeductible Interest

Adding unpaid interest to principal when note is
　renewed
Amortization of bond premium
Charge added in order to pay insurance premiums
　in installments
Debt for which you are not legally liable
Debt to buy stock in a regulated investment company
　if it distributes only exempt-interest dividends
Deductions for unpaid interest by lender from
　principal available for withdrawal
Expenses treated as interest in connection with
　short sale of tax-exempt securities
Interest added to or deducted in advance from life
　insurance loan

Interest paid to carry single-premium life insurance, endowment, or annuity contract

Life insurance loan to fund buy-out plans

Mortgage assistance payments

Penalties or fines paid to any governmental authority, such as for late filing or late payment of taxes

Premium on tax-exempt bonds*

Shareholder's voluntary interest payments on corporate loan

*Can be an adjustment to basis of property

Using the Interest Expense Forms

On the following pages, you'll find forms that allow you to record all deductible interest payments during the year.

Interest Expense Register. Enter your interest payments either as they occur or on a regular basis, such as once a month. If your financial institution doesn't send you a monthly statement showing how your total payment was applied, ask them to provide a monthly breakdown. Do the same with any other loans you've incurred. Enter your yearly totals from the register directly on Schedule A.

Keep all receipts, canceled checks, sales contracts, and other documents in an envelope labeled "Interest Paid." Store it with this book.

Credit Card & Charge Account Interest Paid. On this form you can enter interest and finance charges as shown on your monthly statements. Transfer the total for the year to Schedule A. ■

Interest Expense Register

Date 19 __	Paid to/Reason for Payment	Ck. #, Cash	Home Mortgage Interest					Other Interest Paid					
			Financial Institutions		Individuals		Deductible Points		Auto Loan				
Note: Indicate whether amount is from lender's statement or per a calculation. Retain all data.		**Subtotals**												

56

Interest Expense Register

Date 19 __	Paid to/Reason for Payment	Ck. #, Cash	Home Mortgage Interest			Other Interest Paid		
			Financial Institutions	Individuals	Deductible Points	Auto Loan		
Note: Indicate whether amount is from lender's statement or per a calculation. Retain all data.		**Totals for Year**						

Credit Card & Charge Account Interest Paid

Month	Bank Card	Oil Company Card								Monthly Totals
January										
February										
March										
April										
May										
June										
July										
August										
September										
October										
November										
December										
Totals for Year										

Charitable Deductions

Charitable Contributions

The Internal Revenue Code defines a charitable contribution as a contribution or gift (in money or property) to or for the use of a *qualified* organization. Contributions you actually make before the end of the tax year are deductible only on Schedule A. (Beginning in 1987, charitable deductions are no longer available to nonitemizers.)

This section discusses the typical contributions taxpayers might make in the course of a year, as well as limitations that may apply to your deductions. Record-keeping rules are explained and forms are supplied so you can document your deductions. Problems associated with giving large amounts of money or unusual property to charity are explained as well; since the rules for such gifts are complex, see your tax advisor.

Qualified & Nonqualified Organizations

Qualified organizations are generally those operated solely for religious, educational, scientific, literary, or other charitable purposes, or to foster national or international amateur sports competition or for the prevention of cruelty to animals. Contributions made exclusively for public purposes to a local or state government or to the federal government may also be deductible. Donations to war veterans organizations and nonprofit day-care centers may be deductible, as well.

Here's a brief listing of some qualified organizations:

- Boy and Girl Scouts, Boys Club of America
- Churches, synagogues, and other religious organizations
- Civil defense organizations if created under federal, state, or local law
- Domestic fraternal societies, orders, and associations operating under the lodge system
- Educational organizations (nonprofit only)
- Goodwill Industries, Salvation Army, CARE
- Hospitals and medical research organizations (nonprofit only)

- Public service TV stations
- Red Cross, United Way
- YMCA and YWCA

Nonqualified organizations include private schools that practice racial discrimination in their admissions policy and any organization that loses its tax-exempt status for attempting to influence legislation. And just because an organization is tax exempt doesn't mean that contributions to it are deductible.

Either the organization itself or the IRS can tell you whether it's qualified or not. For all organizations, deductions will *not* be allowed if any part of their net earnings inures to the benefit of any private shareholder or individual.

Deductible Contributions of Money

Rules applying to deductible contributions paid in money are discussed below.

Tax$aver Tip. *The IRS recognizes that it's often impossible to get a receipt when you make regular cash donations, such as while attending religious services. In lieu of a receipt, write down all such donations in the log on page 72 as soon as possible after they're made. Donations should be reasonable in amount; if they're large, it's best to write a check.*

Benefit received for donation. When you make a payment to a qualified organization for the purchase of goods or services or for tickets to a benefit, athletic event, theater, or the like, it's presumed you received something of value in return. Though many taxpayers deduct the entire amount paid, this is not proper under IRS rules. Only the excess you paid *above* the fair market value (FMV), or regular price, is deductible as a contribution, even if you didn't attend the event. If you can't readily determine the FMV, you'll simply have to make a reasonable estimate.

Automobile expenses. At home or away, auto expenses directly related to or for activities benefiting a qualified charitable organization are deductible at the current standard mileage rate of

61

12¢ per mile; or you may deduct your actual costs of gas and oil. Parking fees and tolls are deductible either way. General repairs and maintenance, insurance, and depreciation are *not* deductible. Keep track of your mileage and expenses in the log beginning on page 74.

Other out-of-pocket expenses. When you volunteer your services for charitable reasons, you're never allowed to deduct any amounts for the value of your time or services. But other expenses, such as meals and lodging while away from home overnight, are deductible. You may deduct the travel, meals, and lodging expenses of attending a religious convention, but only if you attend as a chosen representative, not solely as a member.

The IRS has said that the costs of sponsoring cocktail and dinner parties to raise funds and promote an event of a charitable organization are deductible. Also deductible is any clothing you buy that is worn *only* when donating services. Lastly, you can deduct the cost of stationery, postage, and telephone calls connected with your volunteer duties. Use the log on page 73 to record these expenses.

Foster care payments. When you enter into an agreement with a qualified agency to have a foster child (under 19 years old) live in your home, you can deduct the unreimbursed expenses of providing support for the child. They're treated on your return as a charitable contribution to the child-placing agency. There can be *no* profit motive in providing foster care, and, if any reimbursements are received, they reduce the deduction. Include in total support all expenses related to food, lodging, clothing, education, medical and dental care, recreation, and similar necessities.

Other deductible contributions. The following donations made to qualified organizations were found to be deductible:

- Aid to evacuees of a disaster if referred to you by a qualified organization
- Legal expenses if incidental to original gift
- Out-of-pocket expenses for Civil Air Patrol, Civil Defense volunteers, lay ministers, Service Corps of Retired Executives (SCORE), programs to assist unmarried pregnant women
- Pew seats, building fund assessments

- Secretarial and office help for fund-raising mailing
- Tickets donated for resale
- Voluntary amounts withheld from wages for designated charities

Reimbursements. Any reimbursements received for your expenses should be subtracted from your actual expenses before considering any limitations. You may only deduct the excess expenses and, conversely, if your reimbursements exceed your actual expenses, you must include the excess in income in the year received. Record your reimbursements in the log on page 74.

Deductible Contributions of Property

When you donate real or personal property to a qualified organization, your deduction is generally limited to its FMV on the date of the contribution. The rules for determining FMV and for reporting such donations are explained below.

Determining fair market value. Generally, FMV is the price the property would sell for on the open market between a willing buyer and a willing seller under no pressure to buy or sell. To determine and prove your valuation, consider all relevant factors—the cost or subsequent selling price of the property, replacement cost, sales of comparable properties, and the opinions of experts.

Used clothing or furniture. Valuing used clothing or furniture donated to charity can be difficult. Many taxpayers simply deduct a fixed percentage, such as 15% of replacement cost new, but fixed formulas seldom result in an acceptable determination of value because they ignore the *current* value of the item. Though there's still guesswork involved in valuing property, all facts and circumstances have to be considered, including desirability, scarcity, and use.

When you donate used items, try to get a signed, dated receipt from the charity listing all items donated, their condition, and their estimated value at that time.

Tax$aver Tip. *If the organization's receipt is not suitable, ask the recipient to sign,* *date, and value the items directly in the log on page 78. Not only are they the best qualified to assign value, but they're also well aware of the fact that you need documentation. If the item is particularly valuable, such as a fur coat, get an independent appraisal and attach it to your return.*

Cars, boats, and aircraft. To determine the value of a used car, boat, or aircraft, consult the valuation book for that particular vehicle. Such books guide you in making adjustments to the base value for unusual equipment, mileage or use, and general physical condition. For expensive transportation property that you wish to donate, it's wise, and sometimes required (see below), to get an independent appraisal, since the physical condition is critical to the value.

When appraisals are necessary. If the claimed value of donated property exceeds $5,000 ($10,000 for nonpublicly traded securities), you not only

are required to get a qualified appraisal but also must attach an appraisal summary (Form 8283) to your return.

The weight the IRS gives to an appraisal depends on the appraiser's qualifications and knowledge of the property, as well as the completeness of the report. Regardless of who prepares it, the IRS doesn't accept appraisals without question. Thus, the opinion of a person claiming to be an expert is not binding on the IRS, and they are free to make their own determination of FMV or even deny your deduction.

The IRS also has a policy of not issuing any advance rulings either approving or disapproving valuations or appraisals prior to the filing of your return. Clearly, the responsibility for supporting the FMV listed on your return rests solely with *you*.

Though the cost of an appraisal is not deductible as a contribution, you can deduct it as a miscellaneous deduction on Schedule A, subject to a floor of 2% of adjusted gross income (AGI), if the appraisal was related to determining your contribution deduction.

For more information on appraisals, ask the IRS for Publication 561 or consult your tax advisor.

Property that's increased in value. When you donate property of any type and its FMV is greater than its adjusted basis, you may be able to claim a deduction for the full FMV of the property. This will depend on whether it's ordinary income property or capital gains property, or a combination of the two.

Included as ordinary income property are rare books, letters and memoranda, works of art created by the donor, business inventory, stock, and any other short-term capital asset. Your charitable deduction for property of this type is essentially limited to the property's adjusted basis.

If sale of the donated property would have resulted in a long-term capital gain, its full FMV is deductible for charitable purposes.

If you need more information on this topic, ask for IRS publications 526 and 561, or consult your tax advisor.

Nondeductible Contributions

Here's a brief listing of some contributions that are not deductible:

- Donation of use of your property, even if offered rent-free
- Tuition payment to any kind of school, even if a fixed amount, designated as a donation, or a condition of enrollment
- Pre-adoption expenses, though benefits may still be available if requirements for claiming a child as a dependent are met
- Contributions to political parties, candidates, civic leagues, lobbying organizations, and chambers of commerce, though deductions may be claimed for other reasons
- Raffle and bingo expenses, regardless of who receives the money
- Payments to fraternal societies for sickness or burial expenses of members
- Direct contributions to foreign organizations
- Contributions to needy individuals
- Contributions ordered by the court
- Dues, fees, or assessments paid to labor unions, country clubs, lodges, fraternal orders, or similar groups, though deductions may be claimed for other reasons

Limitations on Deductions

The IRS limits the maximum deduction you can take for charitable contributions in any one year. Depending on the type of organization, the deduction may be limited to 50%, 30%, or 20% of your AGI.

The 50% limitation. This limit applies to cash and ordinary income property donated to the following:

1. All public charities
2. All private operating foundations
3. Certain private nonoperating foundations that distribute the contributions they receive to public charities and private operating foundations within 2½ months following the year in which they're received
4. Certain private foundations in which the contributions to a foundation are pooled in a common fund, and the income and principal sum are paid to public charities

The 50% limit also applies to gifts of long-term capital gains property made to such charities if the donor elects to reduce the amount of the deduction by 40% of the capital gains.

The 30% limitation. This limitation applies to gifts of cash or ordinary income property to non-50% foundations and organizations (private nonoperating foundations, public cemeteries, and such organizations as veterans and fraternal groups) and gifts *for the use of* the 50% organizations and foundations.

It also applies to gifts of long-term capital gains property to 50% charities when the donor doesn't elect to reduce the deduction by 40% of the capital gains.

The 20% limitation. Subject to this limitation are gifts of long-term capital gains property to private nonoperating foundations.

Contribution deduction carried over to later years. Donated amounts that you're unable to deduct in the current year because they exceed the applicable AGI limit can be carried forward, with the excess deducted in each of the next 5 years until the entire amount has been claimed. If you have carryovers from more than one year, claim them from the earliest year first. Also, always deduct all allowable contributions for the current year before including contributions carried over from a prior year; then see if the limitations apply.

Whenever you have a carryover, attach a statement to your return for each year, showing the year and amount of the original carryover, how much was claimed in each succeeding year, and how much is still available for future years.

If carryover and limitation provisions apply to you, consult your tax advisor, since the law is quite involved.

When & How to Deduct Charitable Contributions

The timing of claiming deductions for charitable contributions for most taxpayers is much the same as for other types of itemized deductions, with one major exception: you can control when they occur.

When to deduct. You must complete your donations, that is, mail the check or make the credit card charge, before the close of your tax year, typically December 31.

Gifts of properly endorsed stock certificates are completed on the date of mailing or delivery to the charity. But if given to your agent or to the issuing company, the gift is not completed until the stock is transferred on the corporation's books. A promissory note issued and delivered to a qualified organization is not considered as a contribution until you make payments on the note. Also, the granting of an option to buy real property at a bargain price is not a donation until the charity exercises the option.

Tax$aver Tip. *By keeping records of taxable income and expenses during the year, you may be able to project in December if you'll need additional itemized deductions; then you can plan your contributions accordingly. Also, if you expect a decrease in tax rates for the following year, you'll probably want to make contributions before year-end so you can claim more deductions in a year of higher rates.*

If you're short of cash and wish to make cash contributions, you can still claim deductions when you borrow money and use it to make donations.

67

How to report. Itemizers claim charitable contributions on Schedule A. If noncash donations exceed $500, you're required to fill out and attach Form 8283—Noncash Charitable Contributions. If you have obtained an appraisal, you don't have to attach it, but you should retain it with your records. You or your appraiser can complete the form.

Penalties for overstating value. When taxpayers overstate the FMV or adjusted basis of donated property, the IRS assesses a 30% penalty of the underpayment of income tax due to the overstatement. You're generally liable for the penalty if both of the following apply:

1. The amount claimed on the return for either value or adjusted basis is 150% or more of the amount determined to be correct.

2. Because of the overstatement, you underpaid your tax by at least $1,000.

Using the Charitable Contribution Forms

The forms that follow this section will make it easy for you to record the types of donations typically made by taxpayers. Be sure to fill them out completely.

Large Charitable Contributions Paid in Money. Donations made by cash, check, or credit card should be listed here. Be sure to enter the amount donated in the proper limitation column. For contributions totaling $3,000 or more to one organization, include the name and amount directly on Schedule A.

Small Cash Donations. Use this form to record small cash donations you make to any qualified organization during the year.

Other Expenses Related to Charitable Activities. Any expenses you incur related to charitable activities that can't be recorded on any of the other forms can be entered here.

Log of Deductible Travel for Charity Purposes. Keep track here of mileage driven for charitable purposes, both local and away from home. To determine the actual cost of operating your car, keep track of your expenses and divide by the total miles driven during the year. Then multiply by your charitable mileage. If your expenses exceed the standard 12¢-per-mile rate, deduct the higher amount. Keep all receipts and calculations.

Charitable Contributions of Valuable Noncash Property.
If you donate any property of value, complete all
applicable columns. For donations of securities,
record the name of the issuer, the type of security,
and where it's listed. Indicate whether you have a
written document from the recipient, how you
arrived at the FMV, and whether you have an
appraisal.

Make sure you have a copy of any written
agreement with an organization when it relates to
the use (restricted or designated), sale, or other
disposition of the property. If there's no agreement, write out the terms and get the recipient to
sign it.

For contributions of property worth over
$500, you'll need to record how it was acquired.
You should also be able to show how you arrived at
the adjusted basis. Additional information is
required if you're contributing less than the entire
interest in the property during the year.

Donations of Used Personal Items. Record here
information related to donations of used clothing,
furniture, appliances, and the like. ■

Large Charitable Contributions Paid in Money

Date of Contrib.	Qualifying Organization	Ck. #, Cr. Card, or Cash	Under $3,000 Each		All over $3,000 Amount	Grouping for Limitations		
			With Receipts	No Receipts		50%	30%	20%

Large Charitable Contributions Paid in Money

Date of Contrib.	Qualifying Organization	Ck. #, Cr. Card, or Cash	Under $3,000 Each		All over $3,000 ___ Amount	Grouping for Limitations		
			With Receipts	No Receipts		50%	30%	20%
Total from Page 72								
Totals for Year								

Small Cash Donations

Date 19___	Given to	Amount		Date 19___	Given to	Amount		Date 19___	Given to	Amount		Date 19___	Given to	Amount	
											Total for Year (Transfer to Page 71)			

Other Expenses Related to Charitable Activities

Date 19___	Paid to/Description	Ck. #, Cr. Card, or Cash	Tickets for an Event			Office Supplies, Postage, Etc.	Uniforms	Miscellaneous	
			Amount Paid	Fair Market Value	Excess Amt. Deductible		Cost & Upkeep	Description	Amount
	Totals for Year								

Log of Deductible Travel for Charity Purposes

Date 19 __	Destination & Reason for Trip	Standard Mileage Rate Method					Actual Cost Method		Parking Fees & Tolls		Meals & Lodging		Total Expenses		Less Reimb.		Net Deduct. Expense	
		Odometer		Computation															
		Start	End	Miles	Rate	Cost	Gas & Oil								(	)		
					× 12¢										(	)		
					× 12¢										(	)		
					× 12¢										(	)		
					× 12¢										(	)		
					× 12¢										(	)		
					× 12¢										(	)		
					× 12¢										(	)		
					× 12¢										(	)		
					× 12¢										(	)		
					× 12¢										(	)		
					× 12¢										(	)		
					× 12¢										(	)		
					× 12¢										(	)		
					× 12¢										(	)		
					× 12¢										(	)		
					× 12¢										(	)		

Log of Deductible Travel for Charity Purposes

Date 19 __	Destination & Reason for Trip	Standard Mileage Rate Method					Actual Cost Method	Parking Fees & Tolls	Meals & Lodging	Total Expenses	Less Reimb.	Net Deduct. Expense
		Odometer		Computation			Gas & Oil					
		Start	End	Miles	Rate	Cost						
					× 12¢						( )	
					× 12¢						( )	
					× 12¢						( )	
					× 12¢						( )	
					× 12¢						( )	
					× 12¢						( )	
					× 12¢						( )	
					× 12¢						( )	
					× 12¢						( )	
					× 12¢						( )	
					× 12¢						( )	
					× 12¢						( )	
					× 12¢						( )	
					× 12¢						( )	
					× 12¢						( )	
Note: Transfer totals directly to Schedule A.	Totals for Year				× 12¢						( )	

Charitable Contributions of Valuable Noncash Property

Date of Contrib.	Name & Address of Recipient / Where Donation Made	Detailed Description of Property	Type of Contribution (Qualified Conserv., Contribution in Trust, Partial Interest, Etc.)	Restricted (R) or Designated (D)
1/15	Boys Club, San Francisco	100 shares common stock – TPI Co.	Ordinary income property	N/A

Note: Combine the totals from this form and from pages 78–79, and enter that amount on Schedule A.

Support (R) Receipt (L) Letter (O) Other (N) None	Property That Has Appreciated in Value					Complete for Each Noncash Donation over $500			
	Basis or Adjusted Basis	Fair Market Value		Reduce for (O) Ord. Income (C) Cap. Gain	Amount Claimed as Deduction	How Property Acquired	Date Acquired	Original Cost	Current Adjusted Basis
		How Determined	Amount						
R & L	800 00	WSJ/NYSE	1,000 00	(O) (200 00)	800 00	Purchase	9/10/86	800 00	800 00
				( )					
				( )					
				( )					
				( )					
				( )					
				( )					
				( )					
				( )					
				( )					
				( )					
				( )					
				( )					
				( )					
	Totals			( )		Totals			

Donations of Used Personal Items

Acquisition		Description of Item	Condition	Estimated Fair Market Value	Acquisition		Description of Item	Condition	Estimated Fair Market Value
Date	Cost				Date	Cost			

Date of Donation _____ 19____

Organization _____ $ _____

Signed for by _____

Method of Valuation _____

Date of Donation _____ 19____

Organization _____ $ _____

Signed for by _____

Method of Valuation _____

Donations of Used Personal Items

Acquisition		Description of Item	Condition	Estimated Fair Market Value	Acquisition		Description of Item	Condition	Estimated Fair Market Value
Date	Cost				Date	Cost			

Date of Donation _____ 19____

Organization _____ $ ____

Signed for by _____

Method of Valuation _____

Date of Donation _____ 19____

Organization _____ $ ____

Signed for by _____

Method of Valuation _____

Combine with Totals from Page 77.

Casualties & Thefts

Taxpayers who own or have an economic interest in real or personal property often incur losses due to the damage, destruction, or theft of their property. Whether due to a criminal act, an accident, or the vagaries of nature, these losses are subject to certain reductions and limitations which, in effect, allow only major losses to be deductible.

Since they're not treated in exactly the same way, it's important to know the difference between real property and personal property. Real property is, simply, buildings and land. Everything else—clothing, furniture, cars, etc.—is personal property.

Casualty Losses

The IRS defines a casualty as the complete or partial damage, destruction, or loss of property resulting from an event that is sudden, unexpected, or unusual in nature. A *sudden* event is one that is swift and abrupt, not gradual or progressive. An *unexpected* event is one that is ordinarily unanticipated and one that you do not intend to happen. An *unusual* event is one that is extraordinary and not a day-to-day occurrence or typical of the activity in which you were engaged.

Determining the amount of your loss. Only bona fide casualty losses that you actually sustained during the taxable year are deductible. Generally, the casualty loss amount is the lesser of either the property's adjusted basis at the time of the loss or the decrease in its fair market value from immediately before to immediately after the casualty. All losses must then be reduced both by any insurance or other reimbursements received or expected and by any salvage value estimated or received.

The adjusted basis (measurement of investment) in property you own is usually the original cost plus certain additions (such as major improvements) and less some reductions (such as postponed gain on the sale of a home). For most personal items, adjusted basis will simply be the item's original cost.

Casualty and theft losses decrease your basis in the property, since you must subtract the amount of the deductible loss. On the other hand, any money you spend to repair or restore your property will increase the basis. And if your reimbursements are greater than the basis before the casualty occurred, this excess is taxable and is added back to basis.

The *fair market value* (FMV) of property is the price you'd accept from a willing buyer when each of you is aware of all relevant facts with neither being under any pressure to act. For casualty losses, you need to determine how much the property declined in value as a result of the casualty. For this reason, you need to know the FMV of the property both immediately *before* and immediately *after* the casualty occurs. For valuable items, an independent appraisal by a competent, qualified appraiser is always the best way to establish FMV. (See page 64 for information about deducting appraisal fees.)

When determining FMV for real property, the entire property is considered as *one* item. But for casualties to personal property, you must deter-mine values for *each* item; they can't even be grouped into categories. Also, if your property is destroyed by fire or is washed away by a flood, you'll need to compile a list of all lost, damaged, or destroyed items just as a starting point.

> **Tax$aver Tip.** *Take a complete inventory of all your possessions **before** a casualty or disaster occurs. Do it over a period of time, if you like, but develop a concise, detailed listing, using the suggested format on page 90. Store the list in a safe place, preferably away from home, and update it periodically.*

Immediately after a casualty occurs, enter the FMV of all the items on your list. In the absence of other information, enter the amount you would realistically sell an item for both before and after the casualty. In many cases, the value after the casualty will be zero. However, if you later sell damaged items, use the sales price as the value.

There are other acceptable methods for determining the decrease in FMV caused by a casualty. One is to use the actual cost of repairs, but only if the repairs were necessary to restore the property to the same condition it was in prior to the casualty, they weren't excessive and related *only* to the damage from the casualty, and the value of the property after the repairs was about the same as before the casualty.

For automobile casualty losses, check the so-called blue books issued by some automobile organizations. The books can help you determine your car's current value, taking into account mileage and accessories.

If you have a casualty loss on your home, summarize the loss on the form on page 90.

The $100 rule. Once your loss has been reduced by insurance, other reimbursements, and salvage value, there's another reduction you must make: *each* separate casualty must be reduced by $100. This is known as the "$100 rule" and applies *only* to nonbusiness property and to each single casualty event, regardless of the number of property items involved. Closely related events are treated as one casualty.

The 10% rule. After deduction for insurance, salvage value, and the $100 rule, nonbusiness casualties are subject to one final limitation—the 10% rule. It simply means that you can only deduct nonbusiness casualty losses if they exceed 10% of your adjusted gross income (AGI). This limitation applies to the total of all casualty and theft losses for the year. If the net of all these events, because of reimbursements, is a gain, the 10% rule does not apply (see page 88).

Married taxpayers filing jointly are treated as one individual in applying both the 10% and the $100 rules, regardless of who owns the property.

Tax$aver Tip. *When married taxpayers both have a loss from the same casualty or theft, file separately only if you're sure it will result in paying less tax overall. Compute your taxes both ways, jointly and separately, to ensure maximum tax savings.*

83

Disaster area losses. Each year, many taxpayers are adversely affected by such disasters as floods, hurricanes, tornadoes, and the like. Under the Disaster Relief Act of 1974, those taxpayers are provided special tax relief designed to assist them when financial help is needed most. Instead of having to wait until the following January to claim a loss and receive a refund, the law gives you the option of accelerating your casualty loss deduction. You can choose between deducting the loss in the year it actually occurred *or* in the immediately preceding tax year. If the disaster occurred between January 1 and April 15, it's usually best to claim your loss on the prior year's return.

If you have to amend the preceding year's return, use Form 1040X; you figure the amount of the loss under the usual rules, just as if it were sustained in the year before that of the disaster. This means you use your AGI of the *preceding* year for purposes of the 10% limitation. Be sure to reduce the amount claimed by any insurance reimbursements (see page 87).

The regulations say that once you elect to claim a loss in the tax year preceding the disaster, it applies to the entire loss, so you can't split it between two tax years. See your tax advisor about how and when to make this election and about other special rules relating to disaster area losses.

Tax$aver Tip. *Form 1040X, used for amending a return, is designed to expedite your refund, which can help you pay for repairs. To ensure quick processing of your return, whether amended or regular, indicate prominently on page 1 of the return and on the envelope that a disaster loss is being claimed.*

Casualty Deduction Checklist

The following list summarizes deductible and nondeductible casualty losses, according to the IRS and various tax court decisions. Note that certain losses on the nondeductible list are deductible if related to business or income-producing property.

This list is not all-inclusive. If you suffered a loss due to an unexpected, unusual, or extraordinary event not on the list and you understand the rules, claim the deduction.

Deductible Casualty Losses

Accidental loss of property if unavoidable

Airplane and auto accidents

Avalanches, volcanic eruptions

Demolition or relocation of residence ordered due to lack of safety

Earthquakes, even if outside U.S.

Earthslide during construction of residence

Fire, including forest fires

Freeze and frost damage to trees and shrubs

Freezing of auto engine, water pipes

Furniture damaged when dropped by movers

Photographs of casualty (for proof of loss)

Shipwrecks and boat collisions

Snow and ice accumulation

Sonic boom causing damage

Storm damage due to blizzards, dust, floods, hail, hurricanes, ice, lightning, rain, sleet, waves, wind

Termite damage if within 15 months

Vandalism, looting, riots

Water level rise if sudden, tidal waves

Nondeductible Casualty Losses

Accidental dropping of any valuable article

Auto breakdown not caused by collision

Auto damage from potholes or large stones

Baggage and contents lost in transit

Boat damage of others caused by taxpayer

Breakage of property by pet or domestic help

Condemnations of personal-use property

Corrosion, rust, paint oxidation

Defective architectural design in a building

Deterioration over a prolonged period

Driveway cracks due to unstable land

Drought, dry rot, erosion, pollution

Expenses only incidental to casualty

Flood inundation at still-water levels

Injury damages to persons or property

Moth damage (usually to fur coats)

Plant damage by insects, disease, fungus

Rental car cost or repairs while damaged car is being repaired

Residence decline in value due to new highway traffic and noise

Ring unintentionally discarded
Salt water exposure
Temporary quarters due to disaster

Losses from Theft

The courts have held that a theft is a word of broad and general connotation and covers any criminal, unlawful misappropriation of money or property that causes a taxpayer to sustain a loss.

The following events have been found to be thefts, even though some may not be so under the laws of your state:

- Blackmail, burglary, extortion
- Confidence games, swindling
- Embezzlement, misrepresentation
- False pretenses of a criminal nature
- False representation of a material fact with intent to defraud
- Kidnapping for ransom
- Larceny, robbery, threats

This list is not all-inclusive; other similar acts may also be deductible if illegal in your state.

A deductible theft can relate to business, income-producing, or personal use property and generally is subject to the same rules and limitations as casualty losses discussed earlier. Certain subjects presented in the section beginning on the facing page cover both casualties and thefts.

If property you own is stolen, contact a law enforcement agency and your insurance company just as soon as you discover the theft. For tax purposes, it's not required that the police actually investigate the theft.

Lost or mislaid property. Losses from carelessly losing or misplacing money or property are not thefts. Neither are unexplained or mysterious disappearances of property from unknown causes. If there is no positive evidence of breaking or entering and no witnesses saw the theft occur, it will be very difficult to prove your loss.

Determining the amount of loss. Theft losses are determined in the same way that casualty losses are, with one exception. Since you no longer have the property, its FMV after a theft is considered as zero.

First, take the lesser of the property's full FMV or its adjusted basis, both as determined just before the theft; then subtract insurance or other reimbursements received or expected, and deduct $100 for each theft. (Determine adjusted basis and FMV in the same way as for casualty losses.) Finally, combine your theft losses with any other casualty gains or losses. If the result is still a loss, this amount, less 10% of your AGI, is the amount of loss you can claim.

If you get your stolen property back and you haven't filed your return yet, your loss is treated as though a *casualty* loss from vandalism occurred (see page 81 for information on how to determine the amount of the loss).

If the property is recovered in a later year, you'll have to recompute the loss for the year claimed, applying the rules just discussed as well as the $100 and 10% rules. If the refigured loss is less than the amount claimed, you'll have to report the difference as income in the year you recovered the property, unless you received no tax benefits from the loss in the earlier year (see the example on page 88).

When to claim deductions. The code says that "any loss arising from theft shall be treated as sustained during the taxable year in which the taxpayer discovers such loss," which may or may not be the year the theft actually occurred. You deduct the loss—only in the year of discovery—when it can be ascertained with reasonable certainty that there will be *no* recovery or reimbursement.

If the person who misappropriated your property promises to make restitution and there's a reasonable prospect that the payments will be made, there is *no* deductible theft loss. Be sure, however, to get a signed promissory note to that effect. But if the note isn't paid and it becomes obvious it never will be, you're finally rewarded with a tax break, since you can write off the unpaid balance as a bad debt and the $100 and 10% rules don't apply. See your tax advisor for more information.

Other Matters Relating to Casualties & Thefts

The following topics relate to losses from both casualties and thefts.

Reimbursements for casualty and theft losses. Often, the settlement of a claim for reimbursement of a casualty or theft occurs in a tax year after the deduction has been claimed. As stated previously, you must reduce your loss in the year claimed by the amount you expect to recover.

If the amount you actually receive in a later year is *exactly* the same as the amount you reduced your loss by in the previous year, there's no tax effect. But if you receive *less* reimbursement than you expected, you can either claim the additional amount then, along with any other casualty or theft losses you may have, or you can amend the prior year's return and claim the actual final loss amount. Estimate the tax effect of both options to see if it's worthwhile to file an amended return.

It is possible that in a subsequent year you could receive a *larger* reimbursement than the loss you previously estimated and claimed. You do *not* amend the prior year's return; you simply include in income the extra amount received, but only if you received a tax benefit for the deduction in the year claimed. For instance, if the total amount you received was $2,000 but half of your loss was not claimed because of the 10% limitation, you'd only include $1,000 in income in the year received.

A *gain* results when the total of all amounts received *exceeds your adjusted basis* in damaged or stolen property. Gain ordinarily must be reported if you receive unlike property or all cash as a reimbursement. However, you have the option of postponing the reporting of gain if, within a specified time period, you purchase qualified replacement property. Since the rules are complex, see your tax advisor if you have a gain.

Many taxpayers don't file insurance claims for casualty and theft losses because they fear that their premiums may increase or that their policy may even be canceled. Under the provisions of the Tax Reform Act of 1986, you cannot claim a nonbusiness casualty loss deduction unless you file a timely insurance claim.

Property used for both personal and business purposes. Such property is treated as if two separate losses occurred. The allocation is usually made based on the percentage of business use of the property. Apply this percentage to arrive at the business and nonbusiness portions of the loss. The nonbusiness portion is further reduced by the $100 and 10% rules discussed previously.

Net operating losses. An unusually large casualty or theft loss that exceeds your income creates a net operating loss (NOL). An NOL can be beneficial in two ways: it can be carried back and reflected on prior years' returns, resulting in a refund, or it can be carried forward and thereby lower taxes in a future year. Consult your tax advisor to determine which is the best choice for you.

Proving your claims. Record personal or business losses on the form on page 91, transferring totals from the other forms. Also, gather the following information right after the loss occurs:

1. A statement as to the nature and type of casualty, and how the loss was a direct result, with copies of any police or fire reports

2. Proof of ownership of the property or, if leased, that you were contractually liable for the damage

3. A sales contract, lease agreement, or other evidence supporting the purchase price; receipts and canceled checks to support any major additions or improvements

4. Appraisals, insurance adjustors' opinions, or reports showing how the FMV before and after the casualty was determined (for ac-

cidents, this is usually a damage estimate by a qualified person)

5. Photographs showing the extent of damage

6. Receipts for any damage repairs completed

7. For a theft, a copy of the police report proving the theft and showing when you discovered the property missing

Tax$aver Tip. *It's important to prove the original purchase price of your property. If you don't, the IRS will arbitrarily set the amount. In valuing your property, always use the method that gives you the highest value and, of course, the greatest loss. If the amounts you claim are large, attach complete documentation directly to your return to help avoid an audit.*

Reporting your claims. To report casualty and theft losses, transfer the information on the form on page 91 to Form 4684; use Section A for personal casualty and theft losses, Section B for business losses. Claim nonbusiness losses on Schedule A. ■

Suggested Format for Listing Contents of Residence

Description of Item Serial # or I.D. Mark	Condition		Date Acquired	Fair Market Value			Cost or Other Basis	Lesser of Cost or Decrease in FMV
	Before Casualty/Theft	After Casualty/Theft		Before Casualty/Theft	After Casualty/Theft	Decrease after Casualty/Theft		
Stereo #EK102779	Good	Destroyed	9/15/84	500 00	—0—	500 00	1,140 95	500 00
Walnut coffee table	Excellent	Poor	10/5/84	300 00	50 00	250 00	600 00	250 00

Summary of Casualty Loss on Residence

Original Basis of Property Damaged or Destroyed (A)	$	

Increases to Basis		
	$	
Total Additions to Basis (B)		
Adjusted Basis Subtotal (A) + (B)=(C)	$	

Decreases to Basis		
	$	
Total Decreases to Basis (D)	(	)
Adjusted Basis before Casualty (C) − (D) = (E)	$	
Fair Market Values		
Fair Market Value before Casualty	$	
Less Fair Market Value after Casualty	(	)
Decrease in Fair Market Value . . . . (F)	$	
Loss on Residence — Lesser of (E) or (F)	$	

Casualty & Theft Loss Information

Description of Property & Loss — Where Located	Date		1 Cost or Other Basis	2 Depr. Allowed or Allowable	3 Salvage Value if Totally Destroyed	4 Adjusted Basis 1−(2+3)	5 Reimb. Received or Expected	6 Gain, if Applic. (5) − (4)	Fair Market Value			Loss (Lesser of 4 or 9, and Less 5)
	Acquired	Loss or Discovery							7 Before Loss	8 After Loss	9 Decrease (7)−(8)	

Note: Transfer information to Form 4684 (Sec. A for personal losses, Sec. B for business losses). Limitations of $100 and 10% of AGI are reflected on Form 4684.

If asset was used for both business and pleasure, allocate loss based on percentage of business use at time of loss or more recent known percentage.

Moving Expense Deductions

Employees and people who are self-employed can deduct job-related moving expenses, regardless of whether they're just entering the work force, they were transferred, or they quit and found a new job on their own, as long as they satisfy certain tests. Self-employed people must move for legitimate business reasons to qualify for the deduction.

Under the provisions of the Tax Reform Act of 1986, these deductions are now available *only* as itemized deductions, even for the self-employed.

The tests you must meet and the limitations that apply to such deductions are discussed below. At the end of the section, you'll find the forms you'll need to record your moving expenses and travel costs.

Tests You Must Meet

In order to be deductible, your move must be closely related in time and place to beginning work in the new location. The expenses must be incurred within a year from the time you first start working at the new job or business, unless you can prove that extenuating circumstances prevented you from moving sooner. Also, it's usually not considered closely related in place to starting work if the distance from your new home to the new job site is greater than the distance from your old home to the new job location. Despite this rule, a move may be considered closely related in place to the start of work if living in your new home is a condition of employment or if you'll spend *less* time or money commuting because of the move. The homes at both locations must be your principal residence, not a vacation home you own.

Time test. Employees must work full-time for at least 39 weeks during the first 12 months after arriving at the new job location to meet this test. Self-employed people must satisfy this same test and also work full-time for at least 78 weeks during the first 24 months after arrival. Full time

93

is what's considered customary for your type of work, you can work for more than one employer, and you don't have to work 39 weeks in a row. (Failure to meet the time test is discussed later.)

For married couples who both work, only one has to satisfy the full-time work test if they file jointly. Otherwise, each must meet the test and deduct only their *own* expenses.

The time test doesn't have to be met if you're disabled, you're laid off or fired (but not for willful misconduct), or you transfer for your employer's benefit.

Distance test. This test can best be understood if you complete the following:

1. Enter the number of miles from your *former* home to your *new* principal work place: _____
2. Enter the number of miles from your *former* home to your *former* principal work place: (_____)
3. Subtract line 2 from line 1: _____

If line 3 is 35 miles or more, you've satisfied this test. If it's less, you can't claim *any* moving expense deductions. If you had no former

principal place of work, your new job site must be at least 35 miles from your former residence.

Use the shortest route between the locations to figure the distances. Your principal place of work is where you'll spend the most time, where your work is centered, or where you'll work permanently (not temporarily). When you work for more than one employer, your principal work place will depend on time spent, amount of work done, and income earned at each location.

Deductible Expenses

Numerous expenses connected with moving are deductible. They must be reasonable considering the circumstances of your move.

Moving household goods and personal items. Whether you move yourself or hire someone to move you, the cost of packing and moving household belongings from your old home to your new one is deductible. Household members must have lived in the former home *and* in the new one. Included are the costs of shipping your car, storage, and insurance within any consecutive 30-day period from the time your goods are moved out to the time they're delivered.

Travel between old and new residences. The costs of travel, meals, and lodging while en route to your new home are deductible for your entire household, beginning on the day before you actually leave and ending on the day you arrive. Only *one* trip is deductible.

Pre-move house-hunting expenses. If you make house-hunting trips, you can deduct—up to certain limits—the costs of travel, meals, and lodging while you're traveling to and from the new area and also while you're there. However, to be deductible, such trips must take place *after* you've obtained a job in the new area. (For information on deducting job-hunting expenses, see page 109.)

If you're self-employed, you must have made "substantial" arrangements (determined by the IRS on a case-by-case basis) to begin work at the new location. Your attempts to find a new residence need not be successful for the expense to be deductible, and there's no limit on the number of trips you or family members can make.

Temporary living expenses. You can deduct *meal* and *lodging* expenses (up to certain limits) for a 30-day period after you move *if* you're in temporary quarters. However, rent you pay for a home you plan to purchase and any other personal living expenses for you or your family are *not* deductible.

Expenses of disposing of your old home. Deductible as moving expenses are costs (limited in amount) connected with the sale or disposition of your former home, such as escrow, legal and title fees, loan placement charges, points, real estate commissions, state transfer taxes, and the like. Some of these expenses may be taken as an itemized deduction instead. Or you can treat them as selling expenses, which would reduce any gain you had on the sale. (You'll have to decide how to treat each one in view of the limitations and other tax-planning considerations.)

Renters who must end an unexpired lease can deduct all payments related to the early release. Also deductible is the difference between rent you must continue to pay and any rent you receive from subleasing your former home.

Expenses of buying your new home. If you buy a new home, certain acquisition costs, such as appraisals, escrow, and legal and title fees, are deductible as moving expenses (subject to limitations). Or these expenses can be added to the basis. Again, do what works best for you in view of the limitations discussed below. If you lease your new home, you can't deduct any rental payments or security deposits. You can, however, deduct commissions and legal fees associated with acquiring the lease.

Travel by car. To compute moving-related auto expenses, the IRS allows you to use either the standard 9¢ per mile rate, plus parking and tolls, or deduct your actual costs of gas, oil, parking, tolls, and repairs (occurring on the trip). The actual cost method usually results in the larger deduction, but figure it both ways to be sure. No deductions are allowed for depreciation, insurance, or repairs resulting from an accident.

Claiming Your Expenses

Claim moving expenses on Form 3903, either in the year you incurred the expenses or in the year you paid them. However, if you receive any reimbursements or allowances in kind (such as using the company credit card) for your move, it's best to claim the deductions in the same year you receive the reimbursement.

Reimbursements should be reported as income in the year received, and you should be supplied a W-2 form.

Failing to meet the time test. If you deduct the expenses and later on don't meet the time test, you can either amend the prior return, eliminating that deduction and paying additional tax, or simply include the total amount of your previously claimed moving expense deduction in other income in the year you fail to meet the test.

Limitations on deductions. Though there are no limits on the deductibility of amounts spent for moving household goods and traveling to your new home, the combined total of all *other* moving expenses for married people filing jointly, for one working spouse, or for single people can't exceed $3,000, of which no more than $1,500 can be for house-hunting trips and temporary living expenses combined. (If you're married and filing separately, the limitations are half the above amounts.)

Because of these limitations, you need to be very careful about how you classify your expenditures. It's best to consult your tax advisor in order to maximize your deductions.

Different rules apply for members of the armed forces, retired people or survivors, and people on temporary assignments, to name a few. For more information, ask the IRS for Publication 521: *Moving Expenses*.

Using the Moving Expense Forms

The forms described below will help you keep track of all your moving expenses. In addition, you may want to keep a daily diary of all moving-related activities, along with receipts, to provide added substantiation.

Moving Expense Register. This register allows you to categorize your expenses exactly as called for on Form 3903. Make sure you classify your expenses carefully, since certain types are limited, as described above.

Log of Deductible Travel for Moving Purposes. Record all travel, meal, and lodging expenses, being sure to distinguish between house-hunting trips and the actual move itself. Keep receipts for gas and oil and compare your actual expenses with the amount allowable at 9¢ per mile; then use the method that gives you the largest deduction. ∎

Moving Expense Register

Date 19__	Paid to/Description	Ck. #, Cash, or Cr. Card	Moving Household Goods	Temporary Living Expenses	Expenses of Old Home		Expenses of New Home	
					Sale/ Exchange	Rent/Lease	Purchase	Rent/Lease
Totals for Year								

Log of Deductible Travel for Moving Purposes

Date 19 __	Destination & Reason for Trip	Standard Mileage Rate Method					Actual Cost Method	Parking Fees & Tolls	Meals	Lodging		Reim-burse-ments
		Odometer		Computation			Gas & Oil					
		Start	End	Miles	Rate	Cost						
					× 9¢							
					× 9¢							
					× 9¢							
					× 9¢							
					× 9¢							
					× 9¢							
					× 9¢							
					× 9¢							
					× 9¢							
					× 9¢							
					× 9¢							
					× 9¢							
					× 9¢							
					× 9¢							
					× 9¢							
Note: Compute expenses using both methods; use the one that gives you the largest deduction (see page 96).		**Totals for Year**										

Miscellaneous Deductions

Miscellaneous expenses deductible on Schedule A relate primarily to employee business expenses and the expenses of producing income. These deductions have been affected in a major way as a result of the Tax Reform Act of 1986. Effective in 1987, the *total* of all miscellaneous deductions, with a few minor exceptions (see below), is deductible only to the extent that it exceeds 2% of your adjusted gross income. Since this provision will eliminate the deduction entirely for many taxpayers, it becomes increasingly important to claim all the deductions you're entitled to in order to exceed the 2% floor.

Here's a list of the miscellaneous deductions *not* subject to the limitation:

- Impairment-related work expenses for handicapped employees
- Estate tax in the case of income in respect to a decedent
- Certain adjustments where a taxpayer restores amounts held under a claim of right
- Amortizable bond premium
- Certain costs of cooperative housing corporations
- Expenses of short sales in the nature of interest
- Certain terminated annuity payments
- Gambling losses to the extent of gambling winnings

The following sections discuss the expenditures that can be claimed as miscellaneous deductions. At the end are all the forms you'll need to keep track of those deductions, as well as instructions on how to use each one.

Employee Business Expenses

Beginning in 1987, employee business expenses, whether reported on Form 2106 or not, will be claimed on Schedule A as miscellaneous deductions. Outside salespeople who are not self-employed are now treated the same as employees and must also use Schedule A.

Business automobile expenses. If you're an employee required to use a car or any other vehicle in order to properly perform your job duties, you can claim deductions for such use. To determine your expenses, you can choose either the standard mileage rate (SMR), based on a fixed rate established by the IRS, or the actual cost method (ACM), which requires you to keep detailed records and itemize each expense.

Under the Tax Reform Act of 1986, interest on an auto loan is consumer interest subject to the phase-out rules discussed on page 50. It's not an itemized deduction subject to the 2% floor.

The *standard mileage rate method* is the easiest way to figure your deductions. You simply keep track of actual business miles driven during the year, whether locally or away from home, and multiply the total by the rate allowed. Your total deduction simply depends on how many miles you drive. However, you still must record the dates of each use and the business purpose.

Note that you can't use SMR if you lease the car, use it for hire, have claimed accelerated or additional first-year depreciation in a prior year, or

use more than one car in the same business.

The rate currently authorized by the IRS is 21¢ for the first 15,000 business miles and 11¢ per mile thereafter. (Use the 11¢ rate for all business miles if the car is fully depreciated.) This amount is intended to cover most operating and fixed costs, including depreciation. You can also add property taxes, as well as business parking fees and tolls.

Tax$aver Tip. *You may be able to avoid the 2% of adjusted gross income limitation by deducting the business portion of property taxes as taxes, not employee business expenses.*

The *actual cost method* requires you to keep a record of all the actual operating and fixed costs, including depreciation. If a car is used *exclusively* for business purposes, you can deduct *all* the costs. Typically, however, the car is used for both business and personal purposes, so an allocation must be made. Only ordinary and necessary business expenses are deductible.

Computing your auto deduction under ACM is a four-step procedure:

1. Determine the business use percentage (BUP) of your car, usually by dividing total business miles for the year by total miles driven, to see if you meet the 50% test.
2. Determine the total expenses, including depreciation, for the year, exclusive of business parking fees and tolls.
3. Compute a new business use percentage including any investment miles.
4. Multiply your total expenses by that business use percentage, then add parking fees and tolls to determine your deduction for the year.

Though ACM is somewhat more time-consuming, it may result in greater tax savings.

To claim deductions, it's essential to keep accurate and complete records, since you'll be asked directly on Form 2106 if you have written evidence to support your deductions. You'll also be questioned about your BUP and your daily and annual commuting mileage.

Special rules for automobiles placed in service after June 18, 1984, limit annual deductions for depreciation. The Tax Reform Act of 1986 changes the limits for cars placed in service on or after January 1, 1987, to $2,560 the first year, $4,100 the second year, $2,450 the third year, and $1,475 thereafter. In some cases, you're also penalized if business use falls to less than 50% in a subsequent year.

For complete information about auto deductions, see *Sunset's Automobile Tax$aver.*

Away-from-home business travel, meals, and lodging.

Out-of-pocket expenses incurred away from home and related to your trade or business activities are deductible, but only if you're away for more than a day. In order to establish that the trip was an ordinary and necessary business expense, you'll need to keep a log indicating the date of departure and return, the business purpose, and the mileage.

To fully substantiate away-from-home business expenses, save receipts, canceled checks, and other such documentary evidence for all lodging, regardless of the amount, and for other expenditures of $25 or more (not including tips), except for transportation when a receipt is not readily available. Beginning in 1987, unless you're eating alone while away on business, you can deduct only 80% of your business meal expenses, and business must be discussed during, or directly before or after the meal.

Entertainment expenses. Entertainment includes entertaining business associates at restaurants, clubs, theaters, and the like. Deductions may be claimed only if the entertainment is directly related to or associated with your trade or business or if certain exceptions apply. Substantiation requirements are strict: you must be able to prove the elements of amount, time, place, business purpose, and relationship of persons entertained.

In addition to employee expenses being subject to the 2% floor, the Tax Reform Act of 1986 also requires that entertainment deductions be reduced to 80% of the total expenditure.

Business gifts. The costs of business gifts can be deducted if they don't exceed more than $25 given directly or indirectly to any one individual during the tax year. Items that are permanently imprinted with your name, given to numerous business contacts, and cost $4 or less are not subject to the $25 limit.

Business telephone calls. If you make a lot of long-distance business calls from your residential phone, total them from your monthly bill and record them in the Miscellaneous Expense Register.

Business use of home. In order to deduct expenses related to using some portion of a home in a trade or business, very specific tests must be met and some limitations may apply. The rules say that a dwelling unit can be a house, apartment, boat, mobile home, unattached garage, studio, or other similar property that relates to use as living accommodations.

If you're an *employee*, you'll generally have the most difficulty claiming a home office deduction. Even if every other test is met, no deductions will be allowed unless the office is maintained solely for the *convenience of your employer*, not your own convenience. It must be required by your employer and be reasonably related to the nature of your job, not merely appropriate and helpful.

> **Tax$aver Tip.** *Obtain a written policy statement from your employer clearly stating that your office at home is for your employer's convenience, not your own.*

Outside salespeople, starting in 1987, must now claim their home office expenses as a miscellaneous deduction on Schedule A and are subject to the 2% floor. If you're in outside sales and can convert to self-employed status, you can avoid the 2% limitation.

The *exclusive use test* is one of the tests you must meet for this deduction. Simply put, whatever space in your home is specified as being used for your trade or business can't be used for *any* other purpose by you or any members of your family during the taxable year. If you use it for *both* business and personal purposes, your deductions for the business portion of depreciation,

utilities, and the like will automatically be disallowed. The business space doesn't have to be an entirely separate room, however.

The *regular use test,* another test you must meet, can be satisfied by proving that you use the space for business purposes on a regular, continuing basis. Thus, even if the space is not used for *any* other purpose, you'll fail this test if your business use is only incidental or occasional. Your best protection is to document your hours in the log provided for this purpose.

In addition to the first two tests, you must also prove that the business portion of your home meets at least *one* of the following three tests:

1. It must be your principal place of business for *any* trade or business you operate. The word "any" is important here because you're deemed to have a principal place of business for *each* trade or business in which you're engaged. If you have only one trade or business but it's at more than one location, you must determine which is the principal one. If you're an employee, note that the courts have ruled that your employer's principal place of business is not necessarily your principal place of business.

105

2. The business space in your home must be used as a place of business where patients, clients, or customers meet or deal with you in the normal course of business and are physically present on the premises.

3. It's a separate structure used in your trade or business, but not attached to your home, such as a barn, guest house, or detached garage.

Exceptions to the exclusive use test include use of part of your home for either a licensed day-care facility or for the storage of inventory. Day-care services must be provided on a regular basis for children, handicapped persons, or the elderly. Inventory must be stored regularly, and the space must be a specific area, though it can have other uses; also, your home must be the only fixed location for that business.

Determine your business use percentage either by comparing the area used for business with the total square feet of your home or, if the rooms are about the same size, by comparing the number of rooms used for business with the total number of rooms. Apply this percentage against mortgage interest (or rent), real estate taxes, utilities, insurance, repairs that benefit the entire home,

and depreciation. Expenses that benefit only the business part, such as painting a home office, are deducted in full and don't have to be allocated.

To determine your deduction for the business use of your home, use the form on page 130. For more complete information, see *Sunset's Home Office Tax$aver.*

Home computers. If computer equipment is located in your home and you use it for both personal and business purposes, you must keep track of both business and personal use during the year in order to arrive at your business use percentage (BUP); this determines how much of the cost of your computer equipment you can deduct.

Computers placed in service after June 18, 1984, must be used more than 50% for business *each* year or the benefits of accelerated depreciation, Section 179 expense, and investment tax credit (if claimed previously) must be recaptured. However, the Tax Reform Act of 1986 repealed the investment tax credit in most cases retroactive to January 1, 1986, increased the first-year Section 179 write-off to $10,000, and allows computers to be depreciated over a 5-year life under the 200% double declining balance method, providing that the 50% test is met.

Tax$aver Tip. *If you're reasonably sure you can meet the 50% test each year, elect Section 179 and deduct the maximum amount allowed (subject to BUP) the year the computer is placed in service. However, that amount can't exceed the taxable income from the trade or business.*

Even if you never meet the 50% test, you can always deduct depreciation (after applying your BUP) on a straight-line basis over 5 years.

In order for an *employee* to claim any deduction for the business use of a home computer, leased or owned, the use must be for the convenience of the employer and be a required purchase or lease as a condition of employment. By all means, obtain a written statement from your employer. It will be helpful to your case if

employees in similar jobs are also required to purchase or lease a computer.

When it comes to deducting the cost of computer software, you have three options, but your choice must be consistent from year to year. If the purchase price is small (under $100, for example), you can deduct the entire cost in the current year. If the price is significant, deduct the cost over a 5-year estimated life or, if you can establish why this is necessary, over a shorter period.

Tax$aver Tip. *When you purchase software used for business at the same time that you buy hardware, have the cost of the software listed separately. Otherwise, you'll be writing off the software over the same, longer useful life of the hardware.*

If you use Form 4562 to report depreciation, you're required to make some very specific statements directly on your tax return about current deductions for a home computer. You must indicate when it was first placed in service and what the current year's BUP is. You'll also be asked whether you have evidence to support the BUP claimed and if so, if it's written. With good records, you'll reduce the risk of an audit.

Educational expenses. Ordinary and necessary educational expenses related to your job or business are deductible if they're required by your employer, by law or regulations, or to keep your salary, status, or job; or if the course of study maintains or improves skills needed in your job.

Even when you meet the above requirements, you *can't* deduct the expenses if the education is required in order to meet the minimum educational requirements for your trade or business or is part of a program of study that will lead to qualifying you for a *new* trade or business.

Deductions you can claim are amounts spent for tuition, books, supplies, laboratory fees, correspondence courses, tutoring, and research and typing to prepare a paper. If your educational expenses are deductible, you're also allowed to deduct transportation expenses between your general work area and a school located beyond

that area, between where you work and a school within the same general area, and between your home and school if it's not farther than if you traveled from work to school.

To determine your deduction, you can use either the standard mileage rate of 21¢ per mile or the actual cost method. If you're away from home primarily to obtain education, you can deduct the costs of travel, meals, and lodging, but not any expenses for personal activities.

Educational assistance payments received may be tax-exempt; if so, they must be deducted from your educational expenses. Beginning on August 17, 1986, only scholarships for tuition and course-required fees, books, supplies, and equipment for degree candidates are exempt from tax.

When employers provide educational assistance programs to employees under a qualified, separate written plan, the Tax Reform Act of 1986 allows you to exclude from gross income up to $5,250 of amounts paid on your behalf by your employer. Annual amounts that exceed that figure must be included in income. You may not deduct any educational expenses for which you are reimbursed, but you may be able to deduct expenses if they *exceed* the lesser of either the amount reimbursed or $5,250, as long as they meet the other tests for deductibility.

Prior to 1987, taxpayers (primarily teachers) could deduct the expenses for periods of travel directly related to their work. However, the new law eliminates the deduction for travel as a form of education.

Job-hunting expenses. Amounts you spend for travel, transportation, resumés, and employment agency fees are deductible under the following circumstances:

- You look for a *new* job in your *current* occupation, whether you're successful or not.
- You're unemployed and are looking for the *same* kind of work you did for your last employer, but only if a substantial amount of time has not passed.
- You travel to and from a new area primarily to look for a job in your present occupation.
- You travel looking for a job while in the new area, even though the cost of getting there and back is not deductible due to the primary purpose rule above.

- You use your car to visit employment agencies and have resumés prepared or distributed.

The following are *not* deductible job-hunting expenses:

- You look for a job in a new occupation and are successful.
- There's a substantial period of time that you were unemployed and looking for a job.
- You're looking for employment for the first time, even if you're successful.

You may use either the standard mileage rate of 21¢ per mile or the actual cost method to compute your deduction for auto use. If your employer pays you back for an employment agency fee in a later year, you must include it in income if you previously deducted it. You don't have to include in income any fees paid directly by your employer to the employment agency.

Work clothes and uniforms. You can deduct the cost and upkeep of special clothing or equipment *only* if they're required as a condition of your employment *and* they're not suitable for normal everyday use. This includes such protective clothing as hard hats, work gloves, safety shoes, and glasses.

Occupations where deductions for clothing and uniforms not suitable for ordinary use have been allowed include fire fighters, musicians, entertainers, nurses, and transportation workers.

Other employee expenses. Sometimes, employers will give employees who lose their jobs because of lack of work lump-sum income aid payments. If such a payment is included in your income and you're required to pay it back, you can deduct it in the year paid. Dues and initiation fees paid for union membership are deductible, as are assessments for benefit payments to unemployed union members. Not deductible are contributions that provide funds for the payment of sick, accident, or death benefits or contributions to a pension fund.

Other expenses allowed as deductions include dues to professional societies, medical examinations required by an employer, occupational taxes, research expenses of a college professor, small tools and supplies used in your work, and subscriptions to work-related professional journals and trade magazines.

Reimbursed and unreimbursed expenses. When you deduct expenses related to your job, you must also include all reimbursements and allowances on your tax return. In many situations, you'll need to use Form 2106 to report business expenses and reimbursements.

If reimbursement is available but you don't request it, *you lose your deduction forever.* This is because the IRS will not allow you to convert your employer's expenses into a deduction of your own.

When reimbursements are general policy but it's a condition of your employment not to receive any, deductions have, on rare occasions, been allowed. The moral: If you're entitled to reimbursement, request it, even if your employer doesn't pay it.

Even if you're expected to pay certain expenses as a condition of your employment, deductibility for these unreimbursed expenses is *not* assured. There should be a reasonable relationship between the expenditures and your compensation. Get a written statement which says your compensation plan is based on expecting you to incur various business-related expenses.

Keep in mind that, with good records and whether reimbursed or not, you can deduct any job-related expenses necessary to do your job.

Tax$aver Tip. *If you consistently incur expenses and are not reimbursed, discuss with your employer a reduction in salary or commission and replace this decrease with a fixed expense allowance of approximately the same amount. The resultant salary reduction may save some payroll taxes and also help you justify your deductions if you're audited. You must account to your employer, or your allowance will be subject to the usual withholding taxes.*

Expenses of Producing Income

The Internal Revenue Code has a special section for taxpayers who deduct certain ordinary and necessary expenses if paid or incurred for the following reasons:

1. To either produce or collect taxable income

2. To manage, conserve, or maintain property held for the purpose of producing income

3. To determine, contest, pay, or claim a refund of any tax

Your expenses must be directly connected to one of these activities, and the income must be taxable to you. Expenses related to nontaxable income are not deductible. Deductible expenses should be reasonable relative to your overall investment activities.

What is ordinary and necessary? In income-producing activity, an expense is *ordinary* if it's customary, traditional, or usual, and *necessary* if found to be useful, helpful, or proper to the conduct of the investment business. Expenses should also be closely associated with the primary intention of producing income. A good way to prove your intent is to show what resulted from incurring the expense.

Investment clubs. If you're a member of a partnership whose only purpose is to invest in securities that produce taxable income, you can deduct your proportionate share of the partnership's operating expenses.

111

Office expenses. The expenses of maintaining an office (not at home), such as rent, clerical help, supplies, telephone, and depreciation on office furniture, are deductible when related to investment activities. However, investors have not been allowed to claim home office deductions unless the income-producing activity constitutes a trade or business.

Service fees. You can deduct any fees you pay to a bank, broker, trustee, or similar agent to collect taxable interest or dividends. Similarly, custodian fees paid by subscribers in a dividend reinvestment plan are deductible.

Home computer. If you use a computer for the production of income, such as managing investments that produce taxable income, you can deduct a proportionate amount of depreciation. If your business use is limited, avoid the complicated business use rules (see page 106) by depreciating it under the straight-line method.

Legal, tax, accounting, and investment counsel. These fees are deductible when related to producing income. Legal fees for tax advice related to a divorce are deductible if stated separately on the bill; legal expenses to collect taxable alimony are also deductible.

Trustee's administration fees. When these fees are paid in connection with an individual retirement arrangement (IRA) and are billed separately, they are deductible. They're not subject to the annual dollar limit on contributions you can make to an IRA.

Safe-deposit box. The rent paid is deductible only if the box is used to store taxable income-producing stocks, bonds, or investment-related records.

Hobby expenses. Though a hobby is not considered as a business since it's not carried on for profit, expenses associated with it are generally deductible up to the amount of income derived from the hobby. Beginning in 1987, the Tax Reform Act of 1986 says that an activity (other than horse breeding or racing) will be presumed *not* to be a hobby if it's profitable in 3 out of 5 consecutive years.

Gambling losses. These amounts are allowed as a deduction, but you can't deduct more than the amount of your winnings as reported on Form 1040. You must have an accurate diary or other record and be able to prove the amounts of winnings and losses by receipts, tickets, or statements. Also, according to the Tax Reform Act of 1986, the deduction for gambling losses is *not* subject to the 2% floor for miscellaneous deductions.

Other Miscellaneous Deductions

Any amounts paid that assist you in determining the *amount of tax* you owe are deductible in the year of payment. This includes tax advice, planning, and preparation of returns, as well as tax books, such as *Tax$aver*.

Appraisal fees to determine the fair market value of property donated to qualified charitable organizations or to determine the amount of a casualty loss are also deductible when paid.

Nondeductible Expenses

Below is a list of some nondeductible expenses:

- Capital expenditures to buy property with a useful life of more than a year or to increase the value or prolong the life of property

- Check-writing fees charged by a bank for the privilege of writing checks
- Commuting expenses
- Expenses for legal adoption of a child with special needs (effective in 1987)
- Fines or penalties paid to a governmental authority for violating a law or other legal requirement, such as a tax penalty
- Gifts or amounts paid to influence the general public on legislative matters, elections, or referendums
- Insurance premiums for life insurance or for your home, such as fire, liability, or mortgage insurance
- Lunches or other meals while working late or on the weekends
- Personal legal expenses related to property claims and settlement in a divorce, breach of promise suit, or preparation of a will
- Political contributions to a candidate
- Professional accreditation fees
- Stockholders' meetings you attend for companies in which you own stock but have no other interest
- Voluntary unemployment benefit fund contributions to a union or private fund

Using the Forms

The various forms you'll need to record and document your miscellaneous deductions are explained below.

Employee Business Expense Register. Use this register to record, categorize, and total all your deductible employee expenses. Be sure to stay up to date by making entries on a regular basis. If you have large and frequent business expenses, it's wise to maintain a separate checking account. For payments by credit card, wait until you receive your monthly statement, write one check, and distribute the expenses to the proper columns. Get receipts, if possible, for payments made in cash.

> **Tax$aver Tip.** *Pay all bills due for business expenses (except for credit card charges) before year-end so they'll be deductible that year. The law allows you to deduct credit card charges in the year incurred, even if payment occurs the following year. At the end of the year, attach a listing*

114

> *of your employee business expenses to your return, rather than simply showing them as one figure.*

Daily Log of Home Office or Computer Equipment Use. This log will help you record, compute, and document the following figures:

- Total hours the part of your home was used for trade or business purposes
- Total hours your home computer was used for all purposes, as well as for trade or business
- Percentage of business use of your home computer

Use the log to document, in as much detail as possible, that you used the space on a regular basis for business purposes.

When you have a home computer, you must allocate the time it's *actually* used (rather than merely being available for use) between business and personal use. Using the log, record the number of hours the equipment was used for business and investment purposes and the total number of hours it was used for *any* purpose during the year. Compare business hours with the total hours for all uses in order to determine your business use percentage. If it's over 50%, add any investment hours and use that higher percentage to compute your deduction.

Tax$aver Tip. *Review your current BUP often so you can limit personal use, if necessary, to ensure that you meet the 50% test for the year.*

Register of Other Miscellaneous Deductions. Use this register in the same way as the one for employee business expenses. Note that certain home office expenses are deductible based on your percentage of business use, as explained on page 106; expenses that directly benefit the business space are deductible in full.

Computation of Deduction Limitations on Business Use of Home. This form is designed to help you determine if any of the limitation levels apply to you. Depending on the amount of your *net*, not gross, income (effective in 1987), you may be able to deduct all, some, or none of your direct, indirect, and depreciation expenses.

In determining gross income, the starting point in applying the limitations, you may only include income from qualifying business use derived from the business use of your home. When the gross income from your trade or business is derived from more than one location, you have to make an allocation on some reasonable basis. (Use the log beginning on page 122 to help you document your time.)

To determine net income, as required by the Tax Reform Act of 1986, subtract from gross income all business or trade expenses that you would incur regardless of location and that are not subject to allocation or limitation. Transfer this amount to the form and subtract your remaining expenses in the order required by the IRS.

Beginning in 1987, the new law allows home office deductions disallowed because of the income limitations to be carried forward to later years. And remember that any mortgage interest and real estate taxes not claimed as a home office deduction may be deducted on Schedule A. ■

Employee Business Expense Register

Date 19___	Paid to/Description	Check #, Cash, or Cr. Card	Business Automobile Expenses				Away-from-Home Expenses				
			Gas, Oil, Lube	Parking Fees & Tolls	Other Description	Amount	Travel	Meals	Lodging	Other Descrip.	Amount
2/5	1st Nat. Bank/mo. payment	149	88 48	14 00	Water pump repair	123 91	98 00	35 62	52 34	car rental	34 10
	Subtotals										

Business Entertainment		Business Gifts	Business Phone Calls	Educational Expenses		Job-Hunting Expenses		Work Clothes & Uniforms	Trade Journals & Subscrip.	Union Dues		
Description	Amount			Description	Amount	Description	Amount					
Lunch—see receipt	42 75								48 00			

Employee Business Expense Register

Date 19__	Paid to/Description	Check #, Cash, or Cr. Card	Business Automobile Expenses					Away-from-Home Expenses				
			Gas, Oil, Lube	Parking Fees & Tolls	Other			Travel	Meals	Lodging	Other	
					Description	Amount					Descrip.	Amount
		Subtotals										

Business Entertainment		Business Gifts	Business Phone Calls	Educational Expenses		Job-Hunting Expenses		Work Clothes & Uniforms	Trade Journals & Subscrip.	Union Dues		
Description	Amount			Description	Amount	Description	Amount					

Employee Business Expense Register

Date 19__	Paid to/Description	Check #, Cash, or Cr. Card	Business Automobile Expenses				Away-from-Home Expenses				
			Gas, Oil, Lube	Parking Fees & Tolls	Other Description	Amount	Travel	Meals	Lodging	Other Descrip.	Amount
Totals for Year											

Business Entertainment		Business Gifts	Business Phone Calls	Educational Expenses		Job-Hunting Expenses		Work Clothes & Uniforms	Trade Journals & Subscrip.	Union Dues		
Description	Amount			Description	Amount	Description	Amount					

Daily Log of Home Office or Computer Equipment Use

Date 19 __	Description of Use	Hours of Use			Purpose of Use (Allocated by Time)			
		From	To	Total Hours	Trade or Business	Invest-ment	Personal	
1/6	Meeting with C. Bishop re customer mailing	1:30 pm	4:45 pm	3¹/4	3¹/4			
					Subtotals				

Daily Log of Home Office or Computer Equipment Use

Date 19 __	Description of Use	Hours of Use			Purpose of Use (Allocated by Time)			
		From	To	Total Hours	Trade or Business	Invest- ment	Personal	
	Subtotals							

Daily Log of Home Office or Computer Equipment Use

Date 19 __	Description of Use	Hours of Use			Purpose of Use (Allocated by Time)			
		From	To	Total Hours	Trade or Business	Invest-ment	Personal	
		Subtotals						

Daily Log of Home Office or Computer Equipment Use

Date 19 __	Description of Use	Hours of Use			Purpose of Use (Allocated by Time)			
		From	To	Total Hours	Trade or Business	Invest-ment	Personal	
		Totals for Year						

Register of Other Miscellaneous Deductions

Date 19__	Paid to/Description	Ch. #, Cash, or Cr. Card	Business Use of Home									
			Expenses Subject to Allocation & Limitation							Direct Exp. Subject to Limit.	
			Rent	Repairs	Utilities	Insur-ance				Description	Amount
Jan.	Expenses—have receipts	cks. & cash	550 00	85 60	96 09	35 30				Painted office	180 00
	Subtotals										

| Expenses of Producing Income | | | | | | | | Home Computer | | Other | | |
| Investment Club Expenses | | Office Expenses | | Service Fees | Profes-sional Fees | Safe-Deposit Box | | Description | Amount | Tax Help | Appraisal Fees | |
Description	Amount	Description	Amount									
		Supplies	12 39	25 00	50 00	18 00		spread sheet program	29 95			

Register of Other Miscellaneous Deductions

Date 19___	Paid to/Description	Ch. #, Cash, or Cr. Card	Business Use of Home							Direct Exp. Subject to Limit.	
			Expenses Subject to Allocation & Limitation								
			Rent	Repairs	Utilities	Insur-ance				Description	Amount
Totals for Year											

Expenses of Producing Income								Home Computer		Other		
Investment Club Expenses		Office Expenses		Service Fees	Profes-sional Fees	Safe-Deposit Box		Description	Amount	Tax Help	Appraisal Fees	
Description	Amount	Description	Amount									

Computation of Deduction Limitations on Business Use of Home

Net Income from Business Use of Home .... (A) | $ |

Less

Mortgage Interest (X   % BUP) ....

Real Estate Taxes (X   % BUP) ....

Casualty Losses (X   % BUP) ....

    Amount Allowable to Deduct (Total of 3 Prior Lines) .... (B)

    Amount Deducted, Lesser of (B) or (A) .... (C)

Limit on Further Deductions (A) Less (C). If Negative, Stop Here .... (D)

Less Direct & Indirect Expenses Other Than Depreciation

Direct Expenses (from Page 128) ....

Indirect Expenses (from Page 128) ....

    Amount Allowable to Deduct (Total of 2 Prior Lines) .... (E)

    Amount Deducted, Lesser of (E) or (D) .... (F)

Limit on Depreciation Deduction (D) Less (F). If Negative, Stop Here .... (G)

Less Depreciation Expense on Business Part of Home (X   % BUP)

    Amount Allowable to Deduct .... (H)

    Amount Deducted, Less or (H) or (G) .... (I)

Note: Even if (D) or (G) are negative, deductions are allowed for business expenses unrelated to business use of home.

Tax Help

Choosing & Working with a Tax Advisor

Many taxpayers hire a tax advisor to prepare their return. Even if you do your own return, you may need the help of a professional tax advisor to solve a particular problem, to prepare for an IRS audit, or to plan for the future. You'll want to choose a qualified advisor you can trust and work with comfortably and confidently.

Who can be a tax advisor? There are more than 20,000 accounting firms in the U.S., and many thousands of people called tax preparers. Only a handful of states require tax preparers to take classes or be licensed.

It's best to retain someone who can legally represent you at all IRS levels. Generally, this person will be a CPA, an attorney, or an "enrolled agent." An enrolled agent must apply to the IRS, pass an examination, and be approved by the IRS to represent taxpayers. Unenrolled tax preparers may represent their clients *only* at the examination level.

Only CPAs, attorneys, and enrolled agents may perform the following on behalf of any taxpayer:

1. Execute claims for a refund.
2. Receive checks in payment of any refund of taxes, penalties, or interest.
3. Execute consents to extend the statutory period for assessment or collection of a tax.
4. Execute closing agreements with respect to a tax liability or specific matter.
5. Delegate authority or substitute another representative.

Fees paid for these services are deductible. Effective in 1987, taxpayers can only deduct them as a miscellaneous deduction, subject to a 2% floor.

Selecting your tax advisor. Many taxpayers don't take the selection process seriously enough. Be cautious and do your homework before you choose. Remember—if your tax preparer makes a mistake or files your return late, it's *you* who will have to pay any additional taxes, penalties, and interest.

Your goals are to find someone who will charge you a fair fee, not do anything that will cause an audit, and be genuinely interested in maximizing your tax savings. Ask friends or business associates whose tax situations might be similar to yours for recommendations, but don't rely on this alone. Do some investigating yourself, check references, and, above all, ask questions.

Before committing yourself, arrange a brief get-acquainted meeting and ask questions such as these:

- What are your areas of tax specialization?
- How do you keep up to date on tax matters?
- What continuing tax education have you undertaken?
- What is your previous tax experience?

Make sure you feel comfortable with the person but be patient—creating a good working relationship can take time.

If you have difficulty finding a competent professional, contact the American Institute of Certified Public Accountants in New York City or the National Society of Public Accountants in Alexandria, Virginia. They can supply you with names of members in good standing in your immediate area.

Some common pitfalls to avoid include retaining anyone who guarantees you a refund or who urges you to claim deductions to which you know you're not entitled, and hiring anyone who bases their fee on the amount of your refund.

Working with a professional. It's important not to just dump your tax records on your tax preparer's desk and have the preparer organize them for you. It will cost you money in increased fees. For best results, follow these guidelines:

- Present all your records in an orderly manner, categorized and summarized (or as requested by the tax preparer).
- Ask about hourly rates and other expenses of people working on your return, and find out how you might help minimize fees.
- Meet the staff people working on your return.
- Ask to receive copies of any correspondence related to you and ask for explanations for each claimed amount you don't understand.
- Before you sign your return, read each line carefully and compare the figures to your own wherever possible. And *never* sign an incomplete return.

- Make sure the tax preparer signs the return that is filed and that you receive a copy.
- If you're being audited, discuss with your tax advisor beforehand how much of each deduction under review may be allowed. Then you'll know when you can be flexible and when you need to stand your ground.
- Before you receive your tax advisor's final bill, ask that any portion of the bill that is not tax-deductible be detailed, to avoid any IRS disallowances.

Other rules and preparers' penalties. According to the IRS code, tax return preparers are subject to criminal penalties if they make an unauthorized disclosure of tax return information or use such information for any purpose other than to prepare a return. There are also penalties for understatement of taxpayer liability. And penalties are assessable for failing to meet the following requirements, unless the failure is due to reasonable cause and not willful neglect:

1. The return must be signed by the person primarily responsible for preparing the return and must also indicate the preparer's and/or firm's identifying number.

2. At the time the return is presented for signing, the taxpayer must be provided with a completed copy of the final return, though this copy need not be signed by the preparer.

3. For 3 years, preparers must keep available for IRS inspection a record of the name, taxpayer ID number, and principal place of work of each tax preparer who worked for them during the period.

4. Effective in 1985, preparers required to sign returns must advise taxpayers of the substantiation requirements of Section 274(d) of the code, related to travel and entertainment expenses, business gifts, and certain depreciation deductions. Preparers should receive assurances that such substantiation exists, but it need not be in writing.

These and other legal requirements have been established by Congress to protect the public against incompetent and dishonest tax preparers. Your awareness of these requirements can help you protect yourself. ∎

Most taxpayers' contact with the IRS is minimal—they file their return and pay their tax or receive a refund, whichever applies. But subsequently, some taxpayers learn that their return has been selected for an audit for any one of a number of reasons. The sections that follow will help you in this and any other dealings with the IRS.

Filing & Amending Your Return

Often, the procedures for filing a return and amending a previously filed return are not well known. Here is some information that may help you.

Filing your return. Always be sure to fill out your return completely, sign it, and file it on time. There are penalties both for late filing and nonpayment, so even if you can't pay then, be sure to send in your return on time.

If you can't make the filing deadline, you can get an automatic 4-month extension by filing Form 4868 and an additional 2-month extension if you have an acceptable reason. You'll be asked to estimate and pay the tax due when filing the extension. If you can't pay the full tax that's due, the IRS will accept an installment payment plan; you'll need to fill out all the necessary papers and agree to a monthly payment plan.

Filing penalties don't apply to a taxpayer entitled to a refund. Also, penalties for late payment can be waived if you have reasonable cause for not paying your tax when due.

Filing an amended return. Whenever you feel the tax you paid, whether resulting from an audit or some other reason, is excessive or incorrect, you have the right to file a claim for a refund. Check first, however, to be sure that no previous form you signed precludes you from filing such a claim. Individual taxpayers should use Form 1040X to file their claims. If you're amending a return for a prior year, you'll need to attach a copy.

You must file an amended return within 3 years of filing the original return or within 2 years from the date you paid any tax, whichever is later. (If you filed earlier than the due date, it's considered as filed on the due date.)

If you have any complaints about the IRS, call their nearest office to find out where you should write. Two IRS publications which contain a lot of useful information are Publication 910: *Taxpayer's Guide to IRS Information, Assistance, and Publications* and Publication 586A: *The Collection Process (Income Tax Accounts)*.

The Audit & Appeals Process

The job the IRS performs year-round in issuing regulations and tax forms, collecting tax returns and payments, auditing the results, and sending out refunds is indeed awesome. Often, the job is done efficiently and rapidly. But some taxpayers have found just the reverse to be true. Repetitive audits, computer breakdowns, demands for taxes not owed, and misinformation are just some of the complaints taxpayers have made about the IRS.

What you need to learn from this is not to feel threatened if you're being audited by the IRS. As long as you're armed with tax knowledge, good

records, and the necessary documentation, you can feel perfectly confident when questioned. The IRS is much less likely to spend audit time on you than on someone with poor records or no records at all.

How returns are selected for audit. Since an average of only 25 out of every 1,000 tax returns are selected each year, most taxpayers never get audited. Don't think that just because you *are* selected you're suspected of being dishonest. Also don't think that because you received your refund you won't be audited. A look at the information below will help explain the selection process:

1. The majority of all selected returns (approximately 75%) come from a computer program called Discriminant Function System (DIF) which attaches a certain score to every line on your return. The computer compares your return with averages of other taxpayers in your tax bracket and attaches a line-by-line score. The higher your score above their predetermined minimum, the more likely you are to be selected.

2. The Taxpayer Compliance Measurement Program (TCMP) is a totally random-sample

selection process. The sample for the entire nation is small (about 50,000), but you might call it the unlucky lottery system. It's a time-consuming examination where you'll be expected to prove *every* item on your return.

3. In the matching documents method, computers match income information supplied to the IRS on forms (such as the W-2 and 1099) with information on taxpayers' returns.

4. Certain target groups, such as designated occupations and tax shelters, are selected from time to time for auditing.

5. Unusual fluctuations or changes in income or expenses could flag your return for audit. Travel and entertainment expenses have always been a popular audit subject.

6. Tips from informants, often ex-spouses or unhappy ex-employees, can trigger an audit.

7. Repetitive audits are legal as long as the previous one resulted in additional tax due. However, if the same items in a previous year resulted in no change in liability, you can probably get the audit suspended.

If your return shows some unusual or large amounts that you feel could target your return for auditing, attach proof for the amounts directly to your return, along with a narrative explanation. Always make sure all income is declared, so there will be no discrepancy between your return and information already supplied to the IRS. Generally, the IRS can audit your returns for the 3 previous years. If fraud is suspected or no return is filed, it can go back to any year.

How to prepare for an audit. The principal reasons the IRS disallows deductions are incomplete records and inadequate substantiation for claimed expenses. Provide the proof and all you'll need is a lot of patience to survive an audit. It also helps if you can communicate using *their* terms and if you understand tax law as much as possible.

You'll have to decide whether to handle the audit yourself or have a qualified professional represent you. If the issues are simple and the amounts involved are small, try it alone. If not, get help (see page 132 for information on how to select a tax advisor). You should, however, compare the potential tax savings with your advisor's estimated fees. When large amounts of tax are at stake, a professional may achieve a quicker resolution and a more favorable one for you as well.

Regardless of who deals with the IRS, here are some suggestions which will be of help:

1. If possible, insist that the entire matter be handled by correspondence and telephone. This allows you to stick to the issues, avoid personality conflicts, and resolve the audit more quickly.

2. If it must be in person, be familiar with your return, especially the items in question. IRS agents are under a lot of pressure to reach an agreement at the first meeting, so use this to your advantage by bringing everything you might possibly need to prove each item.

3. If the item in question is in a gray area, be aggressive, especially if your records are complete. Argue that you're supplying exactly what the law requires.

4. With prior approval, you can tape-record all meetings, and so can the IRS.

5. And now for the don'ts. Don't try to be buddies with the agent or, conversely, get angry. Don't volunteer any information—just answer the questions. Don't sign anything until you've had a lot of time to review it (with professional help), because once you sign a consent form, there's no appeal.

If you and the agent agree, it's over. If you don't, ask to see the agent's supervisor, who may be easier to deal with in trying to reach a final agreement.

The appeals process. The IRS has established an elaborate system of appeals which offers you a wide variety of options. If you didn't reach an agreement with the agent's supervisor, your next stop, and the only one still within the IRS, is the Appeals Office in your region. It's very informal— you can represent yourself if you like—and most audits are resolved at this level. This is because the appeals officer can bargain with you, so be aware that negotiation will be a constant activity from this point forward. There can be good-faith settlement offers and counteroffers on both sides.

The higher the authority, the more likely the compromise—the IRS wants to settle as much as you. For information about this and other related subjects, ask your local IRS office for Publication 556: *Examination of Returns, Appeal Rights, and Claims for Refund.*

Keep in mind that at any stage of the appeal procedure you can do any of the following:

1. Agree and arrange to pay the tax.
2. Ask the IRS to send you a notice of deficiency in order for you to file a petition with the Tax Court.
3. Pay the tax and immediately file a claim for a refund.

The court system. More and more taxpayers are settling disputes with the IRS through litigation. The number of new cases has more than doubled in the past 5 years, resulting in a large backlog.

The Tax Court will only hear your case if the disputed tax has not been assessed or paid. If it has been paid and you've filed for a refund, you must file suit either in the U.S. District Court or the U.S. Court of Claims. You may represent yourself or have an attorney or someone else admitted to practice before that court represent you.

binding decision can be rendered with a minimum of expense and delay, trial judges have much latitude as to the rules of evidence, and the proceedings are simple and informal.

No formal written opinion is issued, and the decision can't be used as a precedent by other taxpayers. But you give up your right to appeal if the decision goes against you. For a petition form and other information, write to the Clerk of the Court, U.S. Tax Court, 400 Second Street, NW, Washington, D.C. 20217. ■

Tax$aver Tip. *If the dispute involves $10,000 or less (including taxes and penalties) for any one tax year, you can have it handled as a "small tax case." The advantages are that you can represent yourself, a final*

Glossary of IRS Terms

Actual cost method (ACM): A method for claiming automobile operating costs that requires the taxpayer to keep detailed records of each item of expense, including depreciation. The total (not including any parking fees and tolls) is multiplied by the percentage of business use applicable to the car.

Adjusted basis: The actual cost of an asset (basis) plus any additions, such as major improvements made, and less any reductions, such as depreciation claimed.

Adjusted gross income (AGI): Gross income from all sources reduced by certain allowable deductions and losses (but not itemized deductions).

Associated with test: Expenses for entertainment are deductible if considered associated with the active conduct of a trade or business; a clear business purpose in making the expenditure must be established, in addition to its being ordinary and necessary.

Away from home: Any period of time longer than your ordinary work day which includes time for sleep and rest.

Business associate: Any person with whom a taxpayer could reasonably expect to engage or deal in the active conduct of a trade or business, such as a customer, client, employee, partner, or professional advisor, whether established or prospective.

Business entertainment: Covers any business-connected activity generally considered to constitute entertainment, as well as recreation and amusement.

Business relationship test: There must be a proximate relationship to business or to business benefits to meet this test.

Business use percentage (BUP): A percentage determined by dividing business use (either in square footage, miles, or time) by total square footage, miles, or time available for all uses.

Capital expenditure: A major addition or improvement to property that is permanent in nature, increases the value or extends the life of the property, and cannot be deducted in the year incurred (it must be depreciated).

Cash basis method: A method of reporting income only when actually received and deducting expenses only when actually paid.

Convenience of employer test: This test is satisfied if an employer requires an employee to use something as a condition of employment in order to properly perform the employee's duties.

Depreciation: The systematic allocation of the cost of an asset over some period of time, either in equal annual amounts, called straight-line, or at various rates, called accelerated.

Directly related test: Entertainment is considered directly related to business only when all the following requirements are satisfied:

1. At the time, the taxpayer had more than a *general expectation* of deriving income or other business benefit at some future date (not merely goodwill). Income or benefit does not have to result from each entertainment expenditure.
2. During the entertainment period, the taxpayer was *actively engaged* in a business meeting, discussion, or transaction with the person(s) being entertained.
3. The principal purpose of the entertainment was business and not only incidental to it.
4. The money spent was allocable to the person(s) with whom the taxpayer engaged in the active conduct of trade or business during the entertainment.

Employee: Someone subject to the will and control of an employer as to what work is done and when it is done.

Excess itemized deductions: The amount of itemized deductions that exceeded the zero bracket amount (prior to 1987) and was deducted from adjusted gross income.

Exclusive use test: This test is satisfied if the portion of the home being used for business purposes is not used for any other purpose at any time during the taxable year.

Fair market value (FMV): An amount which would influence a willing seller to sell and a willing buyer to buy, each with no pressure to do so.

Improvements: *See* Capital expenditure

Listed property: Depreciable business property used as a means of transportation; any property of a type generally used for purposes of entertainment, recreation, or amusement; and any computer not used exclusively at a regular business establishment.

Ordinary and necessary: An expenditure is *ordinary* if it is a common and accepted practice in a particular trade or business; to be *necessary*, it should be appropriate and helpful in the performance, promotion, or furtherance of a trade or business. *Necessary* does not mean absolutely essential, but it also can't be unreasonable.

Ordinary income: Any income taxed at regular rates and not subject to any preferred tax treatment.

Outside sales: The business of selling and soliciting, away from the employer's place of business, the products or services of the employer.

Placed in service: The date property is in a condition or state of readiness and is available for a specifically assigned use.

Points: A term used to describe charges, usually based on a percentage of the mortgage, paid by the borrower.

Principal place of business: The primary location for conducting business, determined by income earned, time spent, and facilities available at that location.

Principal residence: The home where the taxpayer resides.

Pro rata: A proportionate division or distribution of income or expenses according to some exactly calculable factor, such as a percentage.

Recapture rule: When tax benefits claimed under certain rules for depreciation and investment tax credit have to be paid back because of something that occurs in a later year, such as an early disposition of the property or because the business use percentage 50% test is no longer being met.